Practical English Workbook

Form B

Floyd C. Watkins
Emory University

William B. Dillingham
Emory University

John T. Hiers
Valdosta State College

Houghton Mifflin Company   Boston

Dallas   Geneva, Ill.   Hopewell, N.J.   Palo Alto   London

Stained glass window on cover executed by Susan Heller-Moore and photographed by James Scherer.

Acknowledgment is made to the following sources of reprinted materials:

From Charles Dickens, *Bleak House,* edited with an introduction and notes by Morton Dauwen Zabel. Riverside Editions. Copyright© 1956 by Houghton Mifflin Company. Reprinted with permission.

From *Career Planning: Freedom to Choose* by Bruce Shertzer. Copyright© 1977 by Houghton Mifflin Company. Reprinted with permission.

From *Retailing,* second edition, by Robert F. Hartley, Copyright © 1980 by Houghton Mifflin Company. Reprinted with permission.

Printed in the U.S.A.

ISBN: 0-395-33187-0

Contents

Clauses

Kinds of Sentences

Part 2 Sentence Errors   51

Chapter 3   Common Sentence Errors   52

Sentence Fragments   Comma Splices   Fused Sentences

Chapter 4   Verb Forms   61

Verbs

Tense and Sequence of Tenses   Voice   Subjunctive Mood

Chapter 5   Agreement: Subject and Verb   77

Chapter 6   Pronouns: Agreement and Reference   82

Antecedents   Correct Case

Chapter 7   Adjective or Adverb?   94

Adjectives and Adverbs Compared   Forms of the Comparative and Superlative

Part 3   Sentence Structure   99

Chapter 8   Choppy Sentences and Excessive Coordination   100

Subordination   Completeness   Comparisons   Consistency

Chapter 9   Position of Modifiers, Parallelism, Sentence Variety   121

Modifiers   Dangling Modifiers   Misplaced Modifiers, Squinting Modifiers   Separation of Elements   Parallelism   Sentence Variety

Part 4   Punctuation   147

Chapter 10   The Comma   148

Uses of the Comma   Unnecessary Commas

Chapter 11   Semicolon, Colon, Dash, Parentheses, Brackets   175

The Semicolon   The Colon   The Dash   Parentheses   Brackets

Chapter 12   Quotation Marks and End Punctuation   184

Quotation Marks   End Punctuation

Part 5   Mechanics   191

Chapter 13   The Dictionary   192

Chapter 14   Italics   196

Titles   Foreign Words   For Occasional Emphasis

Chapter 15   Spelling   202

Guides for Spelling   Hyphenation and Syllabication

Chapter 16   Apostrophes, Capitals, and Numbers   218

Apostrophes   Capital Letters   Abbreviations   Numbers

Part 6   Diction and Style   229

Chapter 17   Standard English   230

Improprieties   Idioms   Triteness   Correctness   Wordiness
Repetition

Chapter 18   Connotation, Figurative Language, and Vocabulary   274

Connotation   Figurative Language   Flowery Language

Chapter 19   Paragraph Unity   287

Preface

The organization of the *Practical English Workbook,* Form B, like that of the *Practical English Workbook,* Second Edition, closely follows that of the *Practical English Handbook,* Sixth Edition. For those students who require more practice with basic skills, this workbook is designed to reinforce the instruction of the handbook with parallel lessons, additional examples, and varied exercises. Beginning with parts of speech, the workbook also provides lessons on parts of sentences, sentence errors, punctuation, mechanics, diction and style, and paragraph unity. The logical sequence of these lessons makes the *Practical English Workbook* (Second Edition and Form B) adaptable to other texts as well as to independent study and laboratory instruction for students at all levels.

In both editions the instruction has been greatly expanded. More extensive examples—and full explanations of why an example is correct or incorrect—have been added, and most of the exercises have been completely revised. Sections on the use of the dictionary are new and the lessons on paragraph unity are contemporary and lively. These editions of the *Practical English Workbook* are fundamentally new books. And, while both workbooks are parallel in their coverage, Form B provides a distinct alternative. All its exercises are completely new and draw their material, for the most part, from the world of business and work.

We have attempted to make the style of the workbooks concise and readable and to avoid the extremes of lazy colloquialism and rigid formality. Without being condescending or simplistic, the workbooks stress clarity and precision.

Like the *Practical English Handbook,* the workbooks follow a traditional approach to grammar, punctuation, and syntax. We believe that this method has proven itself over the years the best means to call attention to writing problems and to improve the writing skills of students. This mainstream approach to grammar, punctuation, and syntax has dictated the workbook's methodology. We have worked toward stating the most useful rules in the simplest form possible and have stressed typical problems in both examples and exercises. Throughout the text, emphasis is upon building writing skills and developing the student's understanding of the well-established practices governing the use of the English language.

We are deeply indebted to Professor James O. Williams of Valdosta State College for his aid and advice.

F.C.W.   W.B.D.   J.T.H.

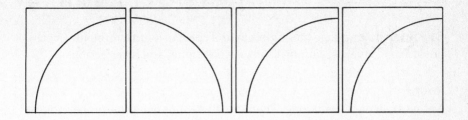

Grammar

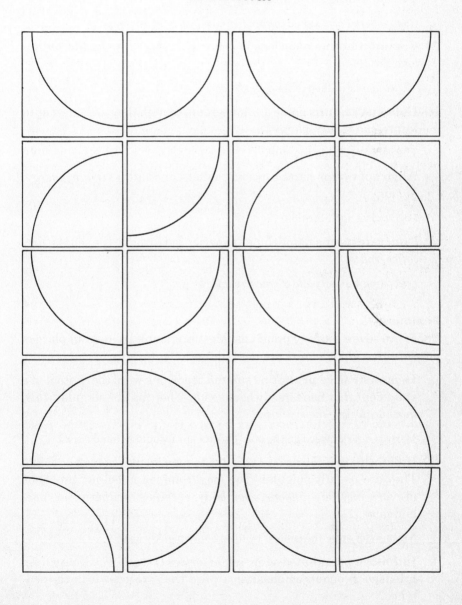

The Parts of Speech 1

The English language has eight parts of speech: nouns, pronouns, verbs, adjectives, adverbs, conjunctions, prepositions, and interjections.

Nouns

Nouns are words that name. There are five kinds of nouns: proper nouns, common nouns, collective nouns, abstract nouns, and concrete nouns.

(a) **Proper nouns** name particular persons, places, or things (Thomas Edison, Chicago, Kleenex).

Commodore Perry sailed to *Japan* on the *U.S.S. Mississippi*.

(b) **Common nouns** name one or more of a class or group *(doctor, pilots, artists)*.

The *students* walked to their *classroom*.

(c) **Collective nouns** name a whole group, though they are singular in form *(senate, jury, clergy)*.

The *herd* is grazing peacefully.

(d) **Abstract nouns** name concepts, beliefs, or qualities *(truth, energy, humor)*.

Loyalty is a noble *virtue*.

(e) **Concrete nouns** name things experienced through the senses *(fire, coffee, roses)*.

I prepared a small *plate* of *crackers* and *cheese*.

Pronouns

There are seven kinds of pronouns. Most pronouns are used in place of nouns, although indefinite pronouns do not refer to any particular noun.

(a) **Demonstrative pronouns** summarize in one word the content of a statement that has already been made. They may be singular *(this, that)* or plural *(these, those)*.

Many people crowded on the bus. *This* meant I would not find a seat.

(b) **Indefinite pronouns** do not indicate a particular person or thing. They are usually singular. The most common indefinite pronouns are *any, anybody, anyone, everybody, everyone, neither, none, one,* and *some*.

Anyone can enter the contest by filling out an entry form.

(c) **Intensive pronouns** end in *-self* or *-selves (herself, themselves)*. An intensive pronoun emphasizes a word that precedes it in the sentence.

She *herself* was surprised at her quick success.

The committee *itself* was confused.

(d) **Interrogative pronouns** *(what, which, who, whom, whose, whoever, whomever)* are used in questions.

Which is mine?

What are we going to do tonight?

(e) **Personal pronouns** usually refer to a person or group of people, but sometimes refer to an object or objects.

We need *her* on the team to help *us* play better.

Put *it* on the table.

	SINGULAR	PLURAL
First person	I, me, mine	we, us, ours
Second person	you, yours	you, yours
Third person	he, she, it, him, her, his, hers, its	they, them, theirs

(f) **Reflexive pronouns** end in *-self* or *-selves* and indicate that the action of the verb returns to the subject.

He caught *himself* making the same mistake twice.

The broken flywheel caused the machine to destroy *itself*.

(g) **Relative pronouns** *(who, whom, whoever, whomever, whichever, whose, that, what, which)* are used to introduce dependent adjective and noun clauses.

You can eat the pie *that is in the refrigerator.* (adjective clause modifying *pie,* introduced by the relative pronoun *that*)

I know *what will help you.* (noun clause used as object of verb *know*)

Verbs

Verbs express an action, a state of being, or a condition.

The bus *screeched* to a stop. (verb showing *action*)

The capital of Missouri *is* Jefferson City. (verb showing *state of being*)

Verbs that show *condition* are called **linking verbs.** The most common linking verbs are forms of the verb *to be (is, are, was, were).* Other linking verbs are *seem, become, look, appear, feel, sound, smell,* and *taste.*

The passengers *were* sleepy. (linking verb showing condition of sleep)

Main verbs may have **auxiliary verbs,** or helpers, such as *are, have, may, will.*

The school band *has* left the field.

Adjectives

Adjectives are descriptive words that modify nouns or pronouns. The **definite article** *the* and the **indefinite articles** *a* and *an* are also classified as adjectives.

The howling dog kept us awake.

Predicate adjectives follow linking verbs and modify the subject of the sentence.

This milk is *sour*.

The dog looks *old*.

Some **possessive adjectives** are similar to pronouns: *my, your, her, his, its, their*. These adjectives refer to specific nouns just as pronouns do but function as adjectives.

Your dinner is ready.

Demonstrative adjectives and demonstrative pronouns have the same forms: *this, that, these, those*. (See demonstrative pronouns, p. 2.)

This comment is helpful. (*This* modifies *comment*.)

This is a helpful comment. (*This* is used here as a demonstrative pronoun.)

Indefinite adjectives resemble indefinite pronouns: *some, many, most, every*.

Every employee received a bonus.

Adverbs

Adverbs describe, qualify, or limit verbs (and verbals), adjectives, and other adverbs.

She left *quickly*. (adverb—modifies a verb)

Talking *fast*, she soon was out of breath. (adverb—modifies the verbal *talking*)

The train was *very* late. (adverb—modifies the adjective *late*)

We'll be through *very* soon. (adverb—modifies another adverb *soon*)

Many adverbs are formed by adding *-ly* to adjectives; others express place or time: *soon, later, always, forever, there, out*.

Take the dog *out*.

Conjunctions

Conjunctions connect words, phrases, and clauses.

Coordinating conjunctions—*and, but, or, nor, for, yet*—connect sentence elements that are of equal rank.

John *and* Mary are visiting us today. (conjunction joining two nouns)

We needed to talk to you, *but* your telephone was always busy. (conjunction joining two independent clauses)

Subordinating conjunctions introduce a dependent element in a sentence—that is, one that cannot stand alone as a sentence. Some common subordinating conjunctions are *although, because, if, since, unless,* and *when*.

When we finished the test. (dependent element, not a sentence)

When we finished the test, we turned in our papers. (dependent element joined to independent clause to form a complete sentence)

We were tired *because we had studied all night.* (dependent element joined to independent clause to form a complete sentence)

Prepositions

Prepositions are connective words that join nouns or pronouns to other words in a sentence to form a unit (called a **prepositional phrase**). Prepositional phrases usually function as either adjectives or adverbs. Some prepositions are *above, at, before, by, from, in, into, of, over, through, up,* and *with*.

The jet flew *through the clouds.* (*Through the clouds* is a prepositional phrase used as an adverb to modify the verb *flew.*)

The woman *in the car* is my mother. (*In the car* is a prepositional phrase used as an adjective to modify the noun *woman.*)

Some words that resemble prepositions function as adverbs:

Go out. (*out* used as adverb)

Go out the door. (*out* used as preposition)

Interjections

Interjections are words that express surprise or strong emotions. They may stand alone or be part of a sentence.

Wow!

Well, you should have been more careful.

Parts of Speech: Nouns   1.1

▶ *Underline the words used as nouns in the following sentences.*

EXAMPLE

Governments must fight inflation continually.

1. Glamour stocks of the past may not be the best buys now.

2. At the end of the path, we found a quiet spot to have our picnic.

3. Production of steel fell dramatically during the last decade.

4. After dinner we flipped a coin to determine who would pay the bill.

5. Urban hotels thrive on large conventions.

6. Marketing through cable television is very effective.

7. A new field of management is the training of supervisors to be more sympathetic leaders.

8. The Consumer Price Index no longer includes the cost of a mortgage on a new home.

9. The Million Dollar Round Table is an association of the best agents of the insurance industry.

10. The golden dome of the state capitol could be seen as much as fifteen miles away.

Parts of Speech: Pronouns   1.2

▶ *Underline the pronouns in the following sentences.*

EXAMPLE

<u>Those</u> <u>who</u> visit the National Archives discover for <u>themselves</u> the living past.
(demonstrative, relative, reflexive pronouns)

1. Although the corporation showed some profits, stockholders were not pleased with the management and replaced them.

2. Making toys is no easy business; it requires inventive talent that consistently can produce new product lines.

3. He spoke to the Downtown Renovation Committee to ask it to include in the proposal money for flower beds and tree plots.

4. One of the multimillion dollar microcomputer companies got its start in someone's garage.

5. Their haste caused them to make too many mistakes.

6. She typed the résumé and sent it off.

7. Whoever makes the best impression will be picked for the position.

8. The document itself was easy to type, but the long tables accompanying it were difficult to follow.

9. She was inclined to buy whatever was advertised on television, even though the prices of these items often were higher than no-name brands.

10. Harold watched the ball as it sailed over the fence.

Parts of Speech: Verbs   1.3

▶ *Underline the verbs in the following sentences.*

EXAMPLE

The astronauts <u>tested</u> many new technological products.

Eventually many <u>were adapted</u> for consumer use.

Space-age research <u>is</u> the source of many household products.

1. Custom-made products cost more.

2. The sales representatives will complete the promotion.

3. We listened to country music on the radio while we drove to work.

4. Condominiums appeal to many busy executives.

5. Can you tell us where we can buy inexpensive linens?

6. The oil slick became larger each day and was now threatening the beaches.

7. One of the paramedics ministered to the stricken man, while the other called the hospital.

8. She needed a larger copier and ordered one with options unavailable just two years ago.

9. Benefits are a continuing contractual concern of American workers.

10. One of the vice presidents of the First State Bank will speak at the convocation this week.

NAME _____

DATE _____   SCORE _____

Parts of Speech: Adjectives   1.4

▶ *Underline the words used as adjectives in the following sentences. Remember that* articles (a, an, the) *are also classified as adjectives.*

EXAMPLE

A good annual report pleases stockholders.

1. The enormous tent outside the department store was filled with new furniture for the big sale.
2. The glass door bore the names of the new officers of the company.
3. Leaving the difficult work for the staff to do later, the supervisor went home for the day.
4. After finishing dinner, we had chocolate cake and vanilla ice cream for dessert.
5. The large truck slowly backed down the long, narrow alley.
6. Rentals are traditionally good, even lucrative tax shelters.
7. The last act of the play was boring, and we left before the curtain came down.
8. An underground economy operates on a totally cash basis.
9. Some employment services use computerized robots to match clients with prospective employers.
10. Conglomerates do not depend on one or two sectors of the general economy for dependable profitability.

Parts of Speech: Adverbs   1.5

▶ *Underline the words used as adverbs in the following sentences.*

EXAMPLE

The rate for treasury bills rose <u>dramatically</u>.

1. Monthly housing costs are higher in Washington, D.C., than in New York City.

2. Lately Ann has seemed especially content.

3. Retail petroleum prices probably will climb again.

4. The officer summarily dismissed the private.

5. "Gold" credit cards usually appeal to one's vanity.

6. Jeff was almost unbeatable when he played video games.

7. Railroads are now almost completely free of regulation.

8. Food prices shift remarkably when computed annually.

9. New orders for durable goods invariably mean a rather stronger economy.

10. At the hastily called press conference, the company's representative answered many particularly difficult questions about the sharp decrease in sales.

Parts of Speech: Conjunctions, Prepositions, and Interjections 1.6

▶ *Underline prepositions in the following sentences once, conjunctions twice, and interjections three times.*

EXAMPLE

"Ah, and that is not all you get," intoned the announcer. "In addition to the set of stainless steel knives and the fruit slicer is this beautiful wooden slicing board."

1. Tardiness is a growing problem among American students and workers, and it is often accompanied by absenteeism.

2. These may be long-standing habits of the workers' past, but through a concentrated effort they can be changed.

3. Some businesses combat the problem with over-hiring.

4. The sum of the numbers in the first column was 378.

5. The county budget was up, but its effect on taxes is not yet known.

6. In the past assuming a mortgage loan was one way of getting a lower interest rate.

7. The president of the local Board of Realtors said, "Oh, we expected the demise of the assumable loan."

8. "All of us are looking forward to the tournament this weekend," the company's newsletter proclaimed.

9. Many companies have an exercise room located at the plant and encourage employee use of it.

10. In some corporations, computer-monitored programs plan and evaluate the fitness needs of employees.

Same Word; Several Functions 1.7

▶ *Many words can function as several parts of speech. Compose very brief sentences with the following words, illustrating the parts of speech in parentheses. If necessary, check a dictionary.*

EXAMPLE

rake (noun) *The hero of the story evolves from a rake to a gentleman.*

rake (verb) *The children raked the field and made a baseball diamond.*

1. form (noun) _____

   _____

   _____

   (verb) _____

   _____

   _____

   (adjective) _____

   _____

   _____

2. even (adjective) _____

   _____

   _____

   (verb) _____

   _____

   _____

   (adverb) _____

   _____

   _____

3. place (noun) _____

_____

_____

(verb) _____

_____

_____

(adjective) _____

_____

_____

4. order (noun) _____

_____

_____

(verb) _____

_____

_____

(adjective) _____

_____

_____

5. stunt (noun) _____

_____

_____

(verb) _____

_____

_____

(adjective) _____

_____

_____

6. paint (noun) _____

_____

(verb) _____

_____

(adjective) _____

_____

7. top (noun) _____

_____

(verb) _____

_____

(adjective) _____

_____

8. reserve (noun) _____

_____

(verb) _____

_____

(adjective) _____

_____

9. back (noun) _____

_____

(verb) _____

_____

_____

(adjective) _____

_____

_____

10. soap (noun) _____

_____

_____

(verb) _____

_____

_____

(adjective) _____

_____

_____

Subjects and Predicates

A sentence has a complete meaning and can stand on its own. Its essential parts are its subject and predicate.

A **subject** does something, has something done to it, or is described.

The *woman* is reading. (subject acting)

Books are read. (subject acted upon)

Books are interesting. (subject described)

A **predicate** says something about the subject.

The woman *is reading*.

Books *are sources of information*.

Books *are interesting*.

The **simple subject** usually consists of one word. The **complete subject** consists of all the words that function together as the subject.

The *house* is dark. (simple subject)

The old house is dark. (complete subject)

When similar units of a sentence are linked together and function together, they are termed **compound.**

The automobile and *the truck* stopped. (compound subject)

The verb in a sentence is called the **simple predicate.** The simple predicate, its modifiers, and any complements are called the **complete predicate.**

Harry *finished* his work. (simple predicate)

Harry *finished his work*. (complete predicate)

Complements

Complements complete the meaning of the sentence. They are predicate adjectives, predicate nominatives, direct objects, and indirect objects. Predicate adjectives and predicate nominatives are also called **subjective complements.**

Predicate adjectives follow linking verbs and describe the subject.

Our neighbor is *tall*. (predicate adjective describing *neighbor*)

The fresh tomato tastes *sweet*. (predicate adjective after linking verb)

Predicate nominatives are nouns that follow linking verbs and rename the subject.

Our neighbor is an *actor*. (predicate nominative renaming neighbor)

Direct objects receive the action of a transitive verb.

We played *scrabble*. (direct object telling what was played)

Indirect objects receive the action of the verb indirectly. When the preposition *to* or *for* is understood, the word is an indirect object. A sentence with an indirect object must also have a direct object.

Sheila gave *me* a present. (indirect object telling *to whom* the present was given)

The Parts of Sentences 2.1

▶ *Underline the simple or compound subjects once and the simple or compound predicates twice. Identify complements with the abbreviations **p.a.** (predicate adjective), **p.n.** (predicate nominative), **d.o.** (direct object), and **i.o.** (indirect object) above the appropriate words.*

EXAMPLE
                       d.o.
Tourists took many photographs of the new office complexes.

1. Silicon chips have revolutionized the electronics industry.

2. Tax reductions may stimulate economic growth.

3. Many service industries thrive during recessions.

4. Pluto may be an escaped moon from the planet Neptune.

5. Public television needs private donations to replace lost federal support.

6. Bluegrass music is popular in large cities throughout the United States.

7. Cable television will be a dynamic growth industry during the next decade.

8. Deregulated airlines offer reduced fares for many flights; however, some of these flights are unprofitable.

9. Imported kerosene heaters are odorless, inexpensive, and efficient.

10. Survey takers provide businesses with much vital information.

The Parts of Sentences 2.2

▶ *Underline the simple or compound subjects once and the simple or compound predicates twice. Identify complements with the abbreviations **p.a.** (predicate adjective), **p.n.** (predicate nominative), **d.o.** (direct object), and **i.o.** (indirect object) above the appropriate words.*

EXAMPLE

$p.a.$
The <u>researchers</u> and <u>photographers</u> <u><u>were</u></u> hungry after the field trip.

1. Government agencies may adopt private business practices in times of financial crisis.

2. The laser scanner brings new speed and clarity to copiers and printers.

3. New home starts were up 1.5 million units over the previous year.

4. America's top corporate executives have influence far beyond the nation's borders.

5. Stocks and bonds are two traditionally popular types of investment.

6. Benefits for outpatient surgery and home care reduce costs for insurance companies and their clients.

7. Coal-fired power plants are probably the cause of some acid rain.

8. Softball has become a professional sport.

9. Many automobile dealers lease new cars and trucks.

10. The chairman of the board gave the stockholders the year's sales figures.

Phrases

A phrase is a group of words that does not have both a subject and verb.

A **noun phrase** consists of a noun and its modifiers.

The new computer programmer started yesterday.

An **appositive phrase** renames a noun.

The Pentagon, *the largest office building in the world,* is located in Washington, D.C.

A **verb phrase** consists of the main verb and its helping verbs.

The house *is being painted*.

Prepositional phrases function as adjectives or adverbs.

The door *to the closet* is open. (adjectival phrase modifying *door*)

The rain fell *in the park*. (adverbial phrase modifying *fell*)

Verbals and Verbal Phrases

A verbal is formed from a verb. Three kinds of verbals are gerunds, participles, and infinitives.

Gerund

A gerund always ends in *-ing* and functions as a noun.

Swimming is fun. (gerund as subject)

Swimming in the high surf after the storm is exciting. (gerund phrase as subject)

Participle

Participles usually end in *-ing, -ed, -d, -t,* or *-n*. They function as adjectives.

Tired of reading, he decided to take a short walk. (modifies *he; tired of reading* is the complete participial phrase)

Troubled by her lack of progress, she decided to replan her time. (modifies *she; troubled by her lack of progress* is the complete participial phrase)

Infinitive

Infinitives begin with *to,* which is followed by a verb. They function as nouns, adjectives, or adverbs.

To show the new student around our school took time. (infinitive phrase as subject)

Camera cases *to be carried on the trip* must be waterproof. (infinitive phrase as adjective)

To be certain of lodging, one should make reservations. (infinitive phrase as adverb)

Phrases 2.3

▶ *On the blank lines, indicate whether the italicized phrase is used as subject, modifier, or verb, and indicate its function in the sentence.*

EXAMPLE

Using credit cards is a way *of life* for modern Americans.

modifier—prepositional phrase modifying noun way.

The scientists, *concerned about the potential hazards,* wanted the latest research findings made public.

modifier—participial phrase modifying noun scientists.

1. Stocks *traded off of the nation's seven stock exchanges* are listed by a new system.

   _____

2. The speaker, a banking executive, warned *of the dangers* of inflation.

   _____

3. She kept her assets *in a wide variety* of investments.

   _____

4. *To export grain* is a major goal of American agriculture.

   _____

5. The administration sent a proposal *to Congress* to prohibit mining and drilling in wilderness areas.

   _____

6. *Speculating in the commodities market,* the broker doubled his client's earnings.

   _____

7. Students participate in business games *to gain experience.*

   _____

8. Downtown areas *are being revitalized* across the country.

   _____

9. Word processors may replace typewriters *in many offices.*

   _____

10. Surgery *with laser beams* is now in the experimental stage.

    _____

32

Phrases   2.4

▶ *Write sentences containing the following words in the prescribed phrases.*

1. *since;* prepositional phrase

   _____

   _____

   _____

2. *with;* prepositional phrase

   _____

   _____

   _____

3. *growing;* gerund phrase used as object of a preposition

   _____

   _____

   _____

4. *granted;* verb phrase

   _____

   _____

   _____

5. *begin;* infinitive phrase used as an object

   _____

   _____

   _____

6. *ascending;* gerund phrase used as subject

   _____

   _____

   _____

7. *end;* infinitive phrase used as a subject

_____

_____

_____

8. *cover;* verb phrase

_____

_____

_____

9. *lecturer;* noun phrase

_____

_____

_____

10. *about;* prepositional phrase

_____

_____

_____

11. *contemplating;* participial phrase

_____

_____

_____

12. *into;* prepositional phrase

_____

_____

_____

13. *converting;* gerund phrase as object of preposition

_____

_____

_____

14. *running;* participial phrase

_____

_____

_____

15. *subway;* noun phrase

_____

_____

_____

16. *going;* verb phrase

_____

_____

_____

17. *remain;* infinitive phrase as an adverb

_____

_____

_____

18. *sparkle;* infinitive phrase as an adjective

_____

_____

_____

19. *under;* prepositional phrase

_____

_____

_____

20. *warned;* participial phrase modifying a subject

_____

_____

_____

Verbals and Verbal Phrases 2.5

▶ *Underline verbals and verbal phrases in the following sentences. Name the verbal, its part of speech, and its function.*

EXAMPLE

<u>Finding his appointment canceled</u>, the sales representative went to Houston.

participle used as adjective to modify noun representative

1. Common sense warned him against stocking too much inventory.

   _____

2. Mounting a strong advertising drive, the company hoped to improve sales.

   _____

3. Finding their place in small businesses, microcomputers are selling very well.

   _____

4. To curb public spending, Yugoslavia phased out food subsidies on cooking oil, meat, and milk.

   _____

5. The apprentice wanted to learn the art of welding.

   _____

6. The couple took courses in management to prepare themselves for another vocation.

   _____

7. One tires of watching television.

   _____

8. Built in the nineteenth century, the courthouse is listed in the *National Register.*

   _____

9. Traveling inexpensively is the subject of many recent books.

   _____

10. Her desire was to become a certified public accountant.

   _____

11. Having made the decision to buy the property, we called the realtor.

_____

12. To manage a portfolio well takes experience, intuition, and intelligence.

_____

13. Given additional time, the clients were able to pay their accounts.

_____

14. Flying is a very safe means of travel.

_____

15. The topics of most columnists seem to be political.

_____

16. Packages to be delivered to local customers must be on the loading dock by noon.

_____

17. The subdivision planner insisted on putting power lines underground.

_____

18. Upon hearing the request, the receptionist hurried the client into the office.

_____

19. After the snowstorm, the farmer began to move his livestock.

_____

20. Railroads continue to provide limited passenger service.

_____

Clauses

Clauses are groups of words with subjects and predicates. Clauses are either independent or dependent.

An **independent clause** can stand alone as a complete sentence. Two or more independent clauses may be linked (1) by coordinating conjunctions *(and, but, or, nor, for)* and a comma, (2) by a semicolon, or (3) by a semicolon and a **conjunctive adverb** (such as *however, therefore, moreover, nevertheless, otherwise*).

The circus is over, **and** the workers are cleaning the grounds. (two independent clauses connected by a comma and a coordinating conjunction)

The river was crowded with barges; each one of them was piled high with coal from the mines of Kentucky and West Virginia. (two independent clauses joined by a semicolon)

Low clouds obscured much of the mountain; **however,** the snow-covered peak sparkled in the bright sunlight. (two independent clauses joined by a semicolon and a conjunctive adverb)

A **dependent clause** may function as a noun, adjective, or adverb.

Who the guest speaker was to be is a mystery. (noun clause as subject)

Anyone *who helps* will be paid. (adjective clause modifying *anyone*)

When the game started, we stood up. (adverb clause modifying *stood*)

Clauses 2.6

▶ *Write whether the dependent clauses are used as nouns, adjectives, or adverbs. Remember that dependent clauses can be parts of independent clauses.*

EXAMPLE

While sales are good, inflation is high.   *adverb*

What the speaker said could not be heard. (dependent clause used as subject of independent clause)   *noun*

15

1. Henry Aaron, *who hit more home runs than any other player,* is now in the Baseball Hall of Fame. _____

2. *Although weekly newspapers are said to be disappearing,* they are still an important part of American life. _____

3. *Whoever plans to be a securities broker* must first pass a difficult state examination. _____

4. *How interest rates may change* is a constant topic among realtors. _____

5. Interstate highways are maintained at great cost *because they are used by so many cars and heavy trucks.* _____

6. Many businesses *which sprang up during the World's Fair* are no longer open. _____

7. Jobs in health care services are available to *whoever has the educational qualifications and the desire to help others.* _____

8. Venus, *which has a surface temperature of over 900 degrees Fahrenheit,* is the third planet from the sun. _____

9. *When Americans turned to smaller cars,* they reduced the consumption of gasoline significantly. _____

10. She called a meeting of all sales personnel immediately *after she learned of the problems.* _____

11. Many older apartment complexes *that are located in inner city areas* have been turned into condominiums. _____

12. China has admitted *that inflation has raised living costs of urban workers.* _____

13. *If economic forecasting is never completely accurate,* it does play an important role for business. _____

14. Urban planning *which is successful* considers the needs of every citizen and group. _____

15. He found his check to be depressingly low *because he forgot about the annuity deduction.* _____

16. She had received two promotions *since she joined the firm.* _____

17. The convention will decide *which candidate to support.* _____

18. We will support *whichever plan is adopted.* _____

19. *When some teachers began permitting students to use calculators,* others predicted that students would soon forget how to perform simple mathematical functions. _____

20. Generic grocery items, *which look like and taste like name-brand products,* are taking a growing share of the consumer dollar. _____

Clauses 2.7

▶ *Write sentences using the following coordinating or subordinating conjunctions or conjunctive adverbs to introduce dependent clauses or to connect independent clauses.*

EXAMPLES

if; to introduce a dependent clause

If the need arises, banks can borrow money from other banks to meet their financial obligations.

and; to connect two main clauses

Overnight express companies are quite profitable, and they are expanding their markets rapidly.

1. *but;* to connect two main clauses

   _____

   _____

   _____

2. *because;* to introduce a dependent clause

   _____

   _____

   _____

3. *which;* to introduce a dependent clause

   _____

   _____

   _____

4. *moreover;* to connect two main clauses

_____

_____

_____

5. *whomever;* to introduce a dependent clause

_____

_____

_____

6. *then;* to introduce a dependent clause

_____

_____

_____

7. *when;* to introduce a dependent clause

_____

_____

_____

8. *yet;* to connect two independent clauses

_____

_____

_____

9. *if;* to introduce a dependent clause

_____

_____

_____

10. *where*; to introduce a dependent clause

_____

_____

_____

Kinds of sentences

There are four kinds of sentences: simple, compound, complex, and compound-complex.

A **simple sentence** has one independent clause.

The President flew to Camp David. (one subject, one predicate)

The President and his advisers flew to Camp David and began work on the budget. (compound subject, compound predicate)

A **compound sentence** contains two or more independent clauses joined by coordinating conjunctions or semicolons.

The new art show at the museum opened today, and the crowd was immense. (two independent clauses joined by *and*)

The new art show at the museum opened today; the crowd was immense. (two independent clauses joined by a semicolon)

A **complex sentence** consists of one independent clause and one or more dependent clauses.

When the new art show at the museum opened, the crowd was immense. (dependent clause and independent clause)

A **compound-complex sentence** is a compound sentence with one or more dependent clauses.

When the play ended, the curtain closed, and the audience applauded loudly. (dependent clause, independent clause, independent clause)

Kinds of Sentences 2.8

▶ *Identify each of the following sentences as simple (s), compound (cd), complex (cx), or compound-complex (cd/cx).*

EXAMPLE

__*S*__ Bombay is the commercial center of India.

_____ 1. Money market funds compound interest daily.

_____ 2. When outdoor advertising is simple and colorful, it is most effective.

_____ 3. Although television was once considered a threat to the publishing industry, talk shows contribute to book sales, and televised movies based on books may cause purchases to soar.

_____ 4. After the real estate broker passes a state examination, he or she may be licensed.

_____ 5. Supermarkets which have good bakeries often have brisk business.

_____ 6. Many business cards include a logo to identify the company visually.

_____ 7. Most students prefer a semester system, although a sizable minority prefer a quarter system.

_____ 8. Automobile manufacturers use more aluminum than in the past, for it is light and durable.

_____ 9. An effective résumé should be concise and clear.

_____ 10. Twenty-four hour cable news channels now broadcast to large audiences, but they began amidst dire predictions that they would fail.

Kinds of Sentences   2.9

▶ *Identify each of the following sentences as simple (s), compound (cd), complex
(cx), or compound-complex (cd/cx).*

EXAMPLE

_CX___ When the alarm rang, everybody rushed out.

_____ 1. Prospective teachers must serve internships.

_____ 2. Salaries vary from one country to the next, but all over the
world medicine is the highest paid profession.

_____ 3. American workers earn more than their counterparts in
other countries, although there are some exceptions, especially among white-collar workers.

_____ 4. If radial tires cost more money, they save gasoline, and they
last longer.

_____ 5. The company publicly announced the merger on June 1.

_____ 6. Recent census figures reveal a population decline in many
urban areas, a reversal of post–World War II trends.

_____ 7. Farm land is decreasing at an alarming rate, and farm profits continue a general decline.

_____ 8. A draftsman has less formal training than an architect, and
he often works under the architect's direction.

_____ 9. Two months after the company announced some layoffs, it
called back most of the workers.

_____ 10. The speaker stressed the need for new employees to be neat,
versed in company policies, and accurate when they re-
spond to clients' questions.

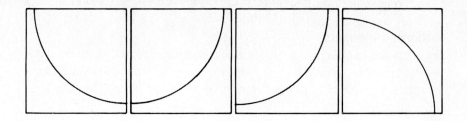

Sentence Errors

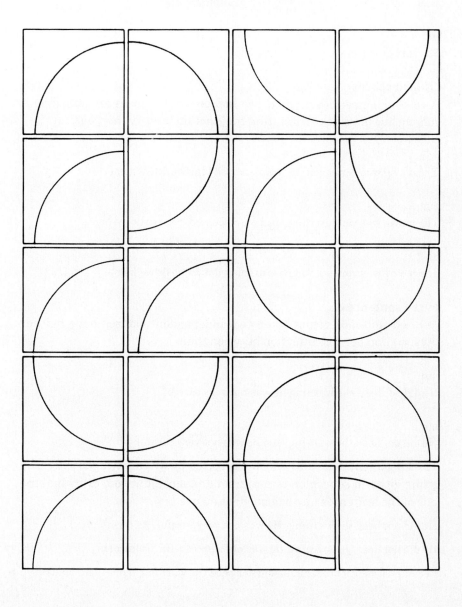

Sentence fragments

Sentence fragments are incomplete sentences and usually consist of dependent clauses, phrases, or any other word group that does not make a complete thought. Fragments should be corrected by making the sentence complete.

NOT

The car being old. (sentence fragment: We bought a new one. (complete sentence)
noun and phrase)

BUT

The car being old, we bought a new one.

Comma splices

A comma splice occurs when two independent clauses are joined by a comma but have no coordinating conjunction *(and, or, nor, but)*.

NOT

The movie was very exciting, we discussed it as we drove home.

BUT

The movie was very exciting, **and** we discussed it as we drove home.

OR

The movie was very exciting; we discussed it as we drove home.

Fused sentences

A fused sentence occurs when two independent clauses have neither punctuation nor a conjunction between them.

NOT

He did not heed the warning he was not very careful.

BUT

He did not heed the warning, and he was not very careful.

Fused sentences also may be corrected by writing two sentences, by using either a semicolon or a comma and a conjunction, or by making one of the sentences into a dependent clause.

He did not heed the warning. He was not very careful. (two sentences)

He did not heed the warning; he was not very careful. (semicolon)

Because he was not careful, he did not heed the warning. (dependent clause)

Sentence Fragments 3.1

▶ *In the blanks at the right identify the following as complete sentences or fragments.*

EXAMPLE

Tune-ups save gas. — *sentence*

Because engines run more efficiently. — *fragment*

1. The cat howling in the backyard. _____

   Prevented our sleeping all night. _____

2. Tax cuts encourage spending. _____

   Which boosts retail sales. _____

3. At last we reached the entrance. _____

   After waiting almost an hour. _____

4. During the last quarter. _____

   Personal spending increased. _____

5. Sales of recreation vehicles declined. _____

   Because the cost of gasoline rose. _____

6. Closely following the counting of votes. _____

   The candidates were uncertain of election. _____

7. Traces of red paint on the worn edges of the chair. _____

   The covering was worn. _____

8. There is no statistical correlation.   —————————

   Between budget deficits and interest rates.   —————————

9. If the Federal Reserve expands the money sup-

   ply.   —————————

   Deficits may cause inflation.   —————————

10. Utility stocks are excellent sources of income.   —————————

   For investors who do not want to speculate.   —————————

Sentence Fragments 3.2

▶ *Correct the following sentence fragments by joining them to the complete sentences.*

EXAMPLE

Banks benefit from deflation, ~~B~~ecause their costs decline faster than their revenue.

1. People first began using ballpoint pens after World War II. Although they were invented in 1888.

2. Being an employee of a union. Legally does not afford one the same protections as union members.

3. Layoffs in Japanese industry are almost unheard of. Because of deeply rooted paternalistic traditions.

4. When overpayments of unemployment benefits occur. Recipients must reimburse the government.

5. My class visited the Highland Park Zoo and the Buhl Planetarium. Before going to a baseball game at Three Rivers Stadium.

6. Freshly made that morning. The pies smelled delicious.

7. Because customers enthusiastically use drive-through windows. Fast-food franchises are increasing sales at them.

8. Although the automobile seemed to run smoothly. We were concerned about a constant whirring sound.

9. Deregulation gives airlines more freedom to set fares. And to change routes.

10. Benefits of deregulation of transportation industries outweigh costs. According to a recent study.

Comma Splices; Fused Sentences   3.3

Comma splices and fused sentences may be corrected in four principal ways:

1. Use a period and write two separate sentences.
2. Use a semicolon between two independent clauses.
3. Use a comma and a coordinating conjunction between two independent clauses.
4. Make one of the clauses dependent.

▶ *Indicate first whether each of the following is a comma splice or a fused sentence. Then in correcting the sentence, indicate the method you used by writing one of the four above numbers in the blank.*

EXAMPLE

Kansas City calls itself the City of Fountains, its goal is to build a new public fountain every year.   *Comma splice / 2.*

1. The ancient biplane taxied to the end of the landing strip it took off and climbed through the clouds.   _____

2. I found an old soft drink bottle behind a country store, I learned from a collector that it was worth twenty-five dollars.   _____

3. Beth visited a new shop named The Attic, she told her friends about it.   _____

4. The copying machine made several bad copies we had to call a repairman.   _____

5. A strange man in a clown suit came to my house and sang a birthday greeting then he realized he was on the wrong street.   _____

6. Procrastination is the single most common error in job-hunting, pursuing the wrong type of prospect is second.   _____

7. Knowledge of nutrition and pharmacology is necessary for the modern nurse they are prerequisites to the study of diet therapy. _____

8. A firm's public relations officer must deal with many publics, hence, he or she must be flexible and courteous. _____

9. Many urban daily newspapers are fighting to survive, on the other hand many suburban dailies are expanding circulation. _____

10. In Venice restoration is the third largest industry it ranks behind tourism and retailing. _____

NAME _____

DATE _____ SCORE _____

Comma Splices; Fused Sentences   3.4

▶ *Indicate whether each of the following is a comma splice or a fused sentence. In correcting the sentence, indicate the method you used by writing one of these four numbers in the blank: (1) corrected with a period (two sentences); (2) corrected with a semicolon; (3) corrected with a comma and a coordinating conjunction; (4) corrected by making one of the clauses dependent.*

1. Aluminum reprocessing is now a major industry, it is cheaper to reprocess used cans than to purchase raw materials. _____

2. The old inn was quite primitive the rooms were heated by fireplaces and lacked bathrooms. _____

3. The second most lucrative profession in the world is the legal profession airline pilots also earn excellent incomes. _____

4. Teachers are in the lowest paid profession worldwide, however, their rewards are often greater than monetary ones. _____

5. Our telephone number is almost identical to that of the library we receive many wrong numbers. _____

6. We bought a new car, we kept the old one for my sister. _____

7. Typical kinds of business communications are memorandums, short reports, and business letters, less typical are long reports and research papers. _____

8. Data processing is an expanding field it pays relatively well and offers chances for promotion. _____

9. A systems analyst must be well versed in all aspects of data processing, he or she must tailor conventional systems to particular businesses. _____

10. A medical transcriptionist need not have a degree in records management one, however, must be a fast, accurate typist. _____

Verb Forms 4

Verbs
All verbs have three **principal parts:**

the **infinitive** *(concern)*

the **past tense** *(concerned)*

the **past participle** *(concerned)*.

These three forms are listed in the dictionary entry of each verb.

Regular, irregular verbs
Verbs may be regular or irregular in form. **Regular verbs** *(add, help, smile)* form the past tense and the past participle by adding -d, -ed, or sometimes -t *(kept, dreamt)*. The principal parts of *add* and *help* are *add, added, added; help, helped, helped.*

    Irregular verbs change form in the past tense and the past participle. Some irregular verbs *(begin, sing)* form the past tense and past participle by changing a single vowel *(sing, sang, sung)*. Other irregular verbs change more than one letter *(drive, drove, driven)*.

Transitive, intransitive verbs
Verbs also may be **transitive** (take an object) or **intransitive** (do not take an object).

TRANSITIVE VERB
The cook *tasted* the special *sauce. (Sauce* is the direct object.)

INTRANSITIVE VERB
The *rain fell* on the roof. *(Fell* does not take an object.)

    Especially troublesome are the irregular verbs *lie, lay; sit, set; rise, raise.* The verbs *lay, set,* and *raise* are transitive and take an object. The verbs *lie, sit,* and *rise* are intransitive and do not take an object.

    Each of these verbs has a specific meaning. *Lie* means to recline or to be situated; *lay,* to place. *Sit* means to be seated; *set,* to place or arrange. *Rise* means to get up; *raise* means to lift. When trying to decide upon the correct form of the verb, think of the meaning you want, whether the verb takes an object or not, the tense you need, and the correct principal part. (See also pp. 71–72.)

Lay the book on the table now. (present tense of *lay*)

She *laid* the book on the table and left. (past tense of *lay*)

The boat *lies* in the harbor. (present tense of *lie*)

The boat *lay* in the harbor for most of last week. (past tense of *lie*)

EXAMPLE

The waiter *set* the plate on the table. (*Plate* is the direct object.)

The archeologist *laid* the relics taken from the temple on the examining table. (*Relics* is the direct object.)

The honor guard will *raise* the flag. (*Flag* is the direct object.)

Some of the swimmers were *lying* on the beach. (*Lying* is intransitive and takes no object.)

The sewing basket was *sitting* in the corner. (*Sitting* is intransitive and takes no object.)

The speaker *rises* to address the meeting. (*Rises* is intransitive and takes no object.)

The principal parts of these verbs are included in the following list of difficult verbs.

Principal parts of some troublesome verbs

INFINITIVE	PAST TENSE	PAST PARTICIPLE
arise	arose	arisen
awake	awoke, awaked	awoke, awaked
be	was	been
bear (to carry)	bore	borne
bear (to give birth)	bore	born, borne
begin	began	begun
bid (offer)	bid	bid
bid (order or say)	bade	bidden
bite	bit	bitten, bit
blow	blew	blown
break	broke	broken
bring	brought	brought
burst	burst	burst
catch	caught	caught
choose	chose	chosen
come	came	come
deal	dealt	dealt
dig	dug	dug
dive	dived, dove	dived
do	did	done
drag	dragged	dragged
draw	drew	drawn
dream	dreamed, dreamt	dreamed, dreamt
drink	drank	drunk
drive	drove	driven
drown	drowned	drowned
eat	ate	eaten
fall	fell	fallen

62

INFINITIVE	PAST TENSE	PAST PARTICIPLE
find	found	found
flee	fled	fled
fly	flew	flown
forget	forgot	forgotten, forgot
freeze	froze	frozen
get	got	got, gotten
give	gave	given
go	went	gone
grow	grew	grown
hang (to execute)	hanged	hanged
hang (to suspend)	hung	hung
have	had	had
hear	heard	heard
know	knew	known
lay	laid	laid
lead	led	led
lend	lent	lent
let	let	let
lie	lay	lain
light	lighted, lit	lighted, lit
lose	lost	lost
pay	paid	paid
pay (ropes)	payed	payed
plead	pleaded, pled	pleaded, pled
prove	proved	proven, proved
raise	raised	raised
ride	rode	ridden
ring	rang, rung	rung
rise	rose	risen
run	ran	run
say	said	said
see	saw	seen
shine (to give light)	shone	shone
shine (to polish)	shined	shined
show	showed	shown, showed
shrink	shrank, shrunk	shrunk
sing	sang, sung	sung
sink	sank, sunk	sunk
sit	sat	sat
slide	slid	slid
sow	sowed	sown, sowed
speak	spoke	spoken
spit	spat, spit	spit, spat
spring	sprang, sprung	sprung
stand	stood	stood
steal	stole	stolen
stink	stank, stunk	stunk
swim	swam, swum	swum

INFINITIVE	PAST TENSE	PAST PARTICIPLE
swing	swung	swung
take	took	taken
tear	tore	torn

Verb Forms 4.1

▶ *Circle the correct verb form. Remember that intransitive verbs do* not *take direct objects. Remember that transitive verbs do take direct objects. Look for both the meaning and tense of the verb.*

EXAMPLE

The secretary (laid, lied) the contract on my desk. (The verb *laid* [past of *lay*] is transitive and takes the direct object *contract*.)

1. Transportation costs (raise, rise) prices in rural communities.

2. The office porter (sets, sits) the daily report on the manager's desk each evening.

3. The tired drivers (laid, lay) briefly on the benches in the rest area.

4. The librarians (lie, lay) the current magazines on tables near the entrance.

5. The patients had (laid, lain) in bed until the nurse left the room.

6. (Sitting, Setting) at the word processor all day may cause eye strain and backache.

7. In South America each office worker goes home for lunch and then (lies, lays) down for a nap.

8. The sun will (raise, rise) at 7:00 A.M.

9. The man (lied, laid) his calculator on the briefcase.

10. Students often (raise, rise) questions after class.

Verb Forms 4.2

▶ *Circle the correct verb form.*

EXAMPLE

Retrieving the morning newspaper, the excited dog unintentionally (tore, torn) several pages.

1. Spotlights (shone, shined) on the World Trade Center.

2. The commodities prices (fell, felled) sharply last week.

3. (Began, Begun) with enthusiasm, the United Way drive was successful.

4. We (hanged, hung) the new drapes for special effects in the lobby.

5. He had (sprang, sprung) new work on his secretary at 4:50 P.M. much too often.

6. Wild swans had (swum, swam) on the lake all morning.

7. Our insurance claim was (paid, payed) within a week.

8. All of the best seats were (taken, took).

9. The rains had (went, gone) quickly.

10. Grand jury members have (born, borne) heavy responsiblities.

Verb Forms **4.3**

▶ *Circle the correct verb form.*

EXAMPLE
The surveyor (drug, (dragged)) the chain across the new lot.

1. On the way to the office, we (swung, swinged) by the dry cleaners.

2. (Led, Lead) by the Federal Reserve Bank, other banks lowered their interest rates.

3. In the hearing, the court allowed the bank to keep the (froze, frozen) assets.

4. Sales had (sunk, sank) to a new low before rebounding.

5. The power company worked all night repairing lines (blown, blowed) down by the high wind.

6. She was (chosen, chose) for membership in the business women's club.

7. He (dugged, dug) through the files hunting for the report.

8. Inflation had (eaten, ate) his raises over the past few years.

9. The angry woman (busted, burst) into the meeting after waiting an hour.

10. The telephone had (rung, rang) all morning in the customer-service office.

Tense and sequence of tenses
Use verbs carefully to express distinctions of time. Avoid needless shifts of tense.

Usually the **present tense** expresses present time.

I *am going* home for lunch.

It also may show repeated action.

I *go* home for lunch.

Past tense shows past time.

I *went* home for lunch.

I *lay* in the sun for an hour. (past tense of verb *lie*)

Future tense shows future time.

I *shall go* home for lunch.

Perfect tenses
The three perfect tenses are used in well-defined sequences. They indicate time or action completed before another time or action.

1. Use **present perfect** with present.

   I *have asked* her to help, and she *refuses*.

2. Use **past perfect** with past.

   He *had wanted* to diet, but he *could* not.

3. Use **future perfect** with future.

   He *will have finished* before we *will begin*.

Infinitive
An infinitive usually takes the present tense when it expresses action that occurs at the same time as that of the controlling verb.

I *desired* to leave.

To complete the project, we *had* to work overtime yesterday.

Relationships between verbs should be logical and consistent.

NOT
I *walk* to the park and *had* lunch. (mixes present tense and past tense)

BUT
I *walked* to the park and *had* lunch. (past tense with past tense)

Voice

When the subject acts, the verb is in the **active voice.** When the subject is acted upon, the verb is in the **passive voice.** Use active voice except on those occasions when passive voice is required.

ACTIVE VOICE

Bill *gave* the book to Mary. (*Bill* acts.)

PASSIVE VOICE

The *book* was given to Mary. (*Book* is acted upon.)

Subjunctive mood

Use **subjunctive mood** to show wishes, commands, or conditions contrary to fact.

I wish I *were* rich. (wish)

The rules require that we *be* silent. (command)

If I *were* vacationing this week, I would be a happy person. (condition contrary to fact)

Tense and Sequence of Tenses 4.4

▶ *Correct the tense of the italicized verbs.*

EXAMPLE

All of these are patterns which c̶a̶m̶e̶ *come* in several variations.

1. Several months *go* by before the architect finished the plans.

2. The office manager will meet with the typing pool, and once again she *praised* the general quality of the typing.

3. Although hardback books last longer than paperbacks, the latter *sold* more copies.

4. Many electricians are surprised *to have encountered* so many cases of unsafe wiring.

5. Not only do rental stores lease furniture and appliances, but several *have sold* them.

6. The dinner we *have* on our flight to Seattle was prepared by a restaurant chain in St. Louis.

7. The contractor *has asked* for a cost overrun, but the state provided none.

8. They will have stopped for the evening before we *will have started*.

9. Most of the staff jog a mile before they *ate* lunch at the office cafeteria.

10. The pilot wished *to have delayed* taking off because of the rain.

Voice 4.5

▶ *In the following sentences change the passive voice to active.*

Pride is instilled and friendships are promoted by voluntary neighborhood clean-up campaigns.

Voluntary neighborhood clean-up campaigns instill pride and promote friendships.

1. The commuter trains were filled with late shoppers.

_____

_____

_____

2. Several preliminary sketches were made by the young draftsman.

_____

_____

_____

3. Since World War II agricultural production has been increased through basic research.

_____

_____

_____

4. Sporting goods stores are expected to profit from the growing popularity of outdoor recreation.

_____

_____

_____

5. Cities may be sued for damages caused by noisy airlines by people living near airports.

_____

_____

_____

6. Telephones are repaired by telephone companies at no charge.

_____

_____

_____

7. Equipment costing thousands of dollars is used by medical technicians.

_____

_____

_____

8. Thousands of trucks are rented by do-it-yourself movers each year.

_____

_____

_____

9. Their security systems are tested regularly by industries holding classified government contracts.

_____

_____

_____

10. Personal bankruptcy claims are filed by an increasing number of individuals.

_____

_____

_____

Agreement: Subject and Verb 5

Use singular verbs with singular subjects, and also use plural verbs with plural subjects. The -s or -es ending of the present tense of a verb in the third person *(he hopes, she stops)* indicates the singular. These endings for most nouns indicate the plural.

After compound subject
A **compound subject** with *and* usually takes a plural verb.

The city *and* the county *are* working together.

Collective nouns
Collective nouns (words like *family, flock, jury*) take a singular verb when referring to a group as a unit; they take a plural verb when the members of a group are treated individually.

My *family is* going on a trip this weekend.

My *family are* going to Hawaii, New Jersey, and Ohio on Labor Day.

After relative pronoun
After a relative pronoun (such as *who, which,* and *that*), the verb in the relative clause has the same person and number as the *antecedent* of the pronoun.

The sales *associate* who *is* here today represents a well-known firm.

After titles
A title of a book or a film is singular and requires a singular verb, even if it contains plural words and ideas.

Elements of Films is a useful book.

After there, here
In sentences that begin with **there** and **here,** the verb agrees with the subject of the sentence.

There *is* an old *mill* on this road.

There *are* many *challenges* in this project.

Word groups
Word groups, such as *in addition to* and *as well as,* do not change the number of the subject when they separate the subject and the verb.

State *officials* **as well as** our mayor *are examining* the problem.

The subject
The *subject* of the sentence, not the predicate noun, determines the number of the verb.

Her main *strength is* her ability to listen and to follow instructions.

When the subject in a sentence is *inverted,* the verb should agree with the *subject* of the sentence, not with the word that comes directly before the verb.

At the party *were Beatrice* and her *sister.* (Plural verb agrees with compound subject.)

Subject and Verb Agreement   5.1

▶ *Underline each subject once; then write the correct verb in the blank at the right.*

EXAMPLE
Periodic <u>tune-ups</u> and oil <u>changes</u> (helps, help) to ensure better gas mileage.

help

1. Some of the management positions for the new plant (is, are) not yet filled.

   _____

2. Chances like this rarely (come, comes) along.

   _____

3. There (is, are) several books that are overdue.

   _____

4. The developer and the architect (was, were) pleasantly surprised with the environmental-impact study.

   _____

5. Here (come, comes) the bands.

   _____

6. Neither the office nor the waiting room (provides, provide) a professional atmosphere.

   _____

7. The fire door at the foot of the stairs (was, were) kept closed at all times.

   _____

8. The water (streams, stream) from the fountain in a high plume.

   _____

9. Learning the routine and observing others on the sales floor (help, helps) new employees feel at ease.

   _____

10. The bookkeeping staff (is, are) meeting at noon.

    _____

Subject and Verb Agreement 5.2

▶ *Underline each subject once; then write the correct verb in the blank at the right.*

EXAMPLE

All video <u>discs</u> (is, are) on sale.   *are*

1. Among those interested in moving to the new mall (was, were) a shoe store and a card shop. _____

2. The polls that (was, were) taken Wednesday indicated that our candidate would win. _____

3. The recreation department and a select group of firefighters (is, are) providing first-aid lessons. _____

4. Sales forces (was, were) called in before the office staff (was, were) told of the merger. _____

5. *Ordinary People* (was, were) an Academy Award winner. _____

6. Horizontal lines and extensive landscaping (make, makes) entrances to office parks inviting. _____

7. The intersection of two major highways (was, were) near the studio offices. _____

8. Spare ribs as well as several salads (was, were) on the menu. _____

9. Workshops on computer programming and sessions with educational consultants (highlight, highlights) the program at the convention. _____

10. On Friday, Margaret and Alicia (go, goes) to the personnel director to have their progress reports evaluated. _____

Antecedents

Use singular pronouns to refer to singular antecedents, and use plural pronouns to refer to plural antecedents. Use a plural pronoun to refer to compound antecedents, except in those cases where the antecedents refer to the same person.

The *instructor* finished grading *her* papers.

The *instructors* finished grading *their* papers.

Which and *that* refer to animals and things. *Who* refers to people and sometimes to animals and things called by name. *That* refers to animals and things, but only sometimes to people.

The refrigerator *that (which)* I bought never needs defrosting.

The representative *who* sold it to me guaranteed the unit for ten years.

Pronouns should not refer vaguely to an entire sentence or to unidentified people. Do not make vague references using pronouns *they, them, it, you,* or *this.*

I have trouble taking standardized tests. *This* is my problem. (*This* is too vague.)

You know that *they* will do *it* every time. (*You, they,* and *it* are vague references.)

Make a pronoun refer clearly to one antecedent only.

UNCERTAIN

The man went to the doctor after *he* finished work. (Does *he* refer to *doctor* or *man?*)

CLEAR

After *he* finished work, the man went to the doctor. (*He* now clearly refers to *man.*)

Correct case

Pronouns have three cases: subjective, possessive, and objective. Personal pronouns and the relative pronoun *who* are inflected for these cases.

Subjective (acting)—I, he, she, we, they, who

Possessive (possessing)—my (mine), your (yours), his, her, (hers), its, our (ours), their (theirs), whose

Objective (acted upon)—me, him, her, us, them, one, whom

To determine case, find out how a word is used in its own clause—for example, whether it is a subject, a subjective complement, a possessive, or an object.

Use the **subjective case** for subjects and subjective complements.

The contractor and *I* are about to reach an agreement. (Use *I*, not *me*, for the subject.)

The winner was *I*. (Use *I*, not *me*, after a linking verb.)

Use the **possessive case** to show ownership and for gerunds.

Their work was complete. (ownership)

Her rising to the presidency reflected hard work. (gerund)

The possessive forms of personal pronouns do *not* have apostrophes.

His is the best solution.

The possessive forms of indefinite pronouns *(everybody's, one's, anyone's)* do have apostrophes. Contractions such as *it's* (for *it is*) and *she's* (for *she is*) do have apostrophes.

Also use the **objective case** for the object of a preposition and for the subject of an infinitive.

Who among *us* will volunteer? (*Us* is the object of *among*.)

The college selected *her* to be the coach. (*Her* is the subject of the infinitive *to be*.)

For interrogative pronouns

The case of interrogatives *(who, whose, whom, what, which* used in questions) depends on their use in a specific clause.

Whom did the Senate confirm for the post? (Use *whom*, not *who*, because the interrogative pronoun is a direct object of *did confirm*.)

For appositives

For pronouns used as **appositives** (words that rename nouns or pronouns) use the same case as the noun or pronoun renamed.

Only we—Sharon and *I*—were excused. (*Sharon* and *I* rename the subject *we*; hence, use *I*, not *me*.)

The instructor excused two of us, Sharon and *me*. (*Sharon* and *me* rename the object of the preposition *of*; hence, use the objective case.)

After *than, as*

The correct case of a pronoun used after *than* or *as* is determined by completing the missing verb of the clause:

Margaret is taller than I. (*Than I am* is the complete clause; *I* is the subject of clause.)

She worked harder than you or I. (*than you or I worked*)

This crisis hurt him more than her. (*more than it hurt her; her* is the object)

Pronouns: Agreement and Reference   6.1

▶ *In the following sentences choose the correct pronouns and write them in the blanks at the right.*

EXAMPLE

"When my clients entered the office, (they, it, one) felt an air of professionalism," said the broker.   *they*

1. All of his business ventures succeeded because (it, they) were planned well.   _____

2. The freshmen law students prepared (their, his) first briefs.   _____

3. The committee submitted (its, their) revised budget.   _____

4. Beaches (which, who) erode easily are poor development sites.   _____

5. We are receiving a good response from national firms (who, which) are making their marketing plans.   _____

6. Many food wholesalers are willing to donate a large quantity of (their, its) inventories to charitable food banks.   _____

7. The physicians (themselves, themself) were anxious about the accumulation of nuclear wastes.   _____

8. The sales representatives discussed (their, one's) competitors' new product lines.   _____

9. Several taxi drivers claimed (their, his or her) profitable fares were from the airport.   _____

10. The woman (who, that) sat next to me at lunch was the vice president for community relations.   _____

Pronouns: Agreement and Reference   6.2

▶ *In the following sentences choose the correct pronouns and write them in the blanks at the right.*

EXAMPLE

(Who, Whom) took that phone call?

Who

1. Public Administration involves applying laws honestly, economically, and efficiently; (it, they) also includes participation in making and interpreting laws.

   _____

2. The crowd boarded the bus for the stadium carrying (their, its) blankets, cushions, and thermos bottles.

   _____

3. The mayor and city manager, whose limited control over the federal program made them feel powerless, expressed (their, her) frustration.

   _____

4. The board members rose to (their, its) feet and applauded the new chairman.

   _____

5. The members of the jury reached (its, their) verdict before lunch.

   _____

6. Special counselors, (who are, which is) employed by the company, have offices on the first floor.

   _____

7. Clothing outlets do not like to store (their, its) summer items for the winter.

   _____

8. Citrus groves were saved from the freeze by owners (which, who) burned smudge pots throughout the night.

   _____

9. Union members marked ballots to choose (those, him or her) who would represent them at the bargaining table.

   _____

10. Recycled glass pays for (itself, oneself) very quickly. _____

Case 6.3

▶ *Write the correct case form in the following sentences in the blanks at the right.*

EXAMPLE

(Whoever, Whomever) invented the small calculator
deserves the gratitude of every finance major.

Whoever

(subject of verb *invented*)

1. The caller asked for me. "This is (she, her)," I told him. _____

2. Honors were bestowed on those (who, whom) sold and listed a million dollars worth of property. _____

3. (His, Him) daydreaming almost made him forget the appointment with his accountant. _____

4. The supervisor considered (her, she) to be an excellent shipping clerk. _____

5. Three of us—Bob, Joe, and (me, I)—plan to attend the conference. _____

6. No technician in the laboratory is as efficient as (she, her). _____

7. To (they, them) go the commissions from the auction. _____

8. The president gave Catherine and (I, me) tickets to Hawaii as a Christmas bonus. _____

9. The travel required in the job was fun for (her, she). _____

10. (Who, Whom) caused the accident we never knew. _____

Case 6.4

▶ *Write the correct case form in the following sentences in the blanks at the right.*

EXAMPLE

(Them, Their) sketches for the advertisement are the ones
we prefer.

Their

1. (We, Us) stenographers attended a seminar on word processing.

   _____

2. Photographers like (us, we) have the most difficult assignments.

   _____

3. The airlines told (us, we) that our reservations were confirmed for all segments of the business trip.

   _____

4. The travel agent told my vice president and (I, me) that changing our plans now would be difficult.

   _____

5. We could not hear the speaker because of (their, them) whispering.

   _____

6. The buyers, most of (whom, who) had years of experience, received frequent job offers from competitors.

   _____

7. Many economists believe that (we, us) taxpayers must pay too much money to the government.

   _____

8. The governor traveled to Japan with three aides and (I, me) in search of industry.

   _____

9. We helped more than (they, them), but they received more credit.

   _____

10. My accountant and (I, me) often confer.

    _____

Case 6.5

▶ *Write the correct case form in the following sentences in the blank at the right.*

EXAMPLE

Voted best brokers were Linda and (I, me).   _____~I~_____

1. Mr. Smith said, "It is (I, me) who called last night."   _____

2. The design came from (I, me) as well as from several other commercial artists.   _____

3. My family was as excited as (I, me) when I bought my microcomputer.   _____

4. We sent the memorandum to (whoever, whomever) was interested in the training program.   _____

5. Upon (them, their) signing the contract, the new owners assumed full liability for accidents on the property.   _____

6. The recipients of the scholarships were (they, them).   _____

7. The nurse trainee, searching for directions on burn care, found (them, they) on page 356.   _____

8. (Whoever, Whomever) desires a career in accounting must have at good background in mathematics.   _____

9. My business partner, for (who, whom) I have the highest regard, rarely beats me at golf.   _____

10. The mediator asked the labor negotiator and (her, she) to return after a break.   _____

Adjectives and adverbs compared

Adjectives modify nouns and pronouns. **Adverbs** modify verbs, adjectives, and other adverbs.

The bright light hurt *our* eyes. (*The* and *bright* are adjectives modifying *light,* and *our* is a possessive adjective modifying *eyes.*)

The news spread *quickly.* (*Quickly* is an adverb modifying *spread.*)

Most adverbs end in *-ly.* Only a few adjectives (*lovely, friendly,* for example) have this ending. Some adverbs have two forms, one with *-ly* and one without (*closely, close* and *quickly, quick*). Most adverbs are formed by adding *-ly* to adjectives (*sudden, suddenly* and *hasty, hastily.*)

We had an *easy* choice to make. (*Easy* is an adjective.)

We made the choice *easily.* (*Easily* is an adverb.)

Use a predicate adjective, not an adverb, after a linking verb, such as *be, become, seem, look, appear, feel, sound, smell, taste.*

The *meat* tastes *bad.* (*Bad* describes the *meat.*)

The *actress* felt *calm.* (*Calm* describes the *actress.*)

One feels *good* after finishing a long swim. (*Good* describes how one feels.)

BUT

After treatment, the patient feels *well.* (Adverb *well* describes a state of health.)

Forms of the comparative and superlative

Use the **comparative form** of the adjective to refer to two things; use the **superlative form** to refer to more than two. Add *-er* or *-est* to form the comparative and the superlative of most short modifiers.

The new air terminal is much *larger* than the old one.

Of the five hotels in our city, the *newest* one is the *largest.*

Use *more* or *most* (or *less* or *least*) rather than *-er* and *-est* before long modifiers, that is, modifiers of several syllables.

He is *more capable* than his brother. (not *capabler*)

He is the *most capable* person I know. (not *capablest*)

He is very *fast.* (predicate adjective)

He is *faster* than his brother. (comparative form)

He is the *fastest* runner in our class. (superlative form)

Some adjectives and adverbs have irregular comparative and superlative forms:

good, better, best: bad, worse, worst

NAME _____

DATE _____ SCORE _____

Adjective or Adverb?   7.1

▶ *Write the correct form of adjective or adverb in the blank at the right.*

EXAMPLE
A series of (high, highly) productive sales promotions attracted new accounts.

highly

(adverb *highly* modifies adjective *productive*)

1. The wholesalers found joint advertising to be
   (real, really) effective.   _____

2. The fashion show went as (good, well) as the de-
   signers had hoped.   _____

3. The last cash register tested was the (slowest,
   slower) of the three.   _____

4. The large number of entries in the trade fair was
   (especially, especial) gratifying.   _____

5. Soft music created a (delightful, delightfully) atmosphere for the typing pool.   _____

6. Lloyd's of London probably is the (most, more)
   famous of insurers.   _____

7. The (bright, brightly) lit office contained the
   firm's conference table.   _____

8. The clerk was praised by the manager for not be-
   having (rude, rudely) to the angry consumer.   _____

9. The workers hammered (loud, loudly) outside
   the receptionist's office.   _____

10 The technical writer's clear directions made as-
   sembly (easy, easily).   _____

Adjective or Adverb?   7.2

▶ *Write the correct forms of adjectives or adverbs in the blanks at the right.*

EXAMPLE

The window display looks (good, well).   *good*

(adjective *good* after linking verb)

1. The apprentice plunged (eager, eagerly) into the
   work.   _____

2. Traffic for Friday was (normal, normally).   _____

3. Using the (quick, quickly) solved problem as
   proof of their computer's superiority, the young
   investors asked for the banker's support.   _____

4. Of the two layouts, the freeform and the grid pat-
   tern, I like the freeform (best, better).   _____

5. My friend from Peru could not understand why a
   dime was smaller than a penny if the penny had
   the (smaller, smallest) value.   _____

6. He thought they were (inadequate, inade-
   quately) prepared to work as junior executives.   _____

7. The new engines whispered (quiet, quietly) as
   the new jetliner soared.   _____

8. Our new location improved customer traffic
   (great, greatly).   _____

9. Safety engineers worked (close, closely) with
   production personnel to test the dangers of some
   forms of insulation.   _____

10. My partner approached the venture (uneasy,
    uneasily), but I knew we would do well.   _____

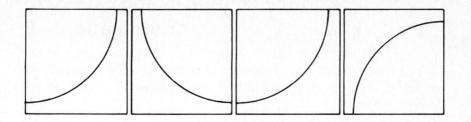

Sentence Structure

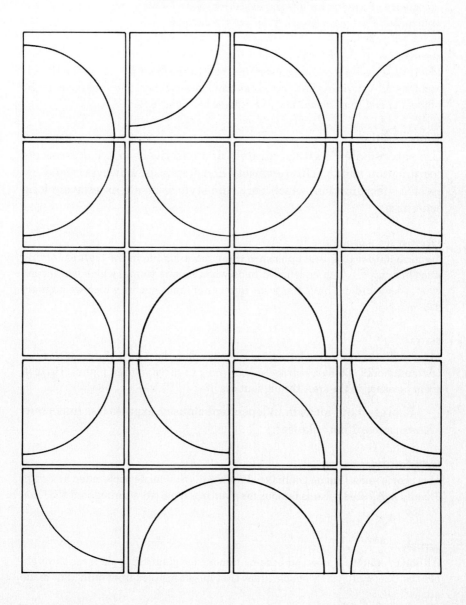

Choppy Sentences and Excessive Coordination   8

Linking a number of short dependent clauses and sentences produces wordiness and monotony and fails to show precise relationships between thoughts.

EXAMPLE
The United States has changed significantly in the last fifty years, for the life expectancy of Americans has increased ten years for men and fifteen years for women, and the nation's work force has quadrupled.

IMPROVED
The United States has changed significantly in the last fifty years. The life expectancy of Americans has increased ten years for men and fifteen years for women. In addition, the nation's work force has quadrupled.

Subordination

Use subordinate clauses accurately and effectively to avoid excessive coordination and to achieve variety and emphasis. However, avoid excessive subordination, which may ruin style or create excessively long sentences.

EXCESSIVE SUBORDINATION
My grandfather took great pleasure throughout his life in the craft of carving wooden figures, which he learned to do when he was young, which was a time when people did not have the great number of amusements which we have today.

BETTER
My grandfather, who lived in a time when people did not have the great number of amusements of today, learned when young to carve wooden figures. He took great pleasure in the craft throughout his life.

Express main ideas in independent clauses; express less important ideas in subordinate clauses.

IMPROPER SUBORDINATION
Few people know that he got his seed from mills that made apple cider, although Johnny Appleseed became famous for planting apple trees throughout the Ohio Valley.

BETTER
Although Johnny Appleseed became famous for planting apple trees throughout the Ohio Valley, few people know that he got his seed from mills that made apple cider.

Avoid excessive overlapping of subordinate clauses. A series of clauses with each one depending on the previous one is confusing.

The United States Treasury Department, which is located in Washington, which is responsible for the printing and minting of currency, is also responsible for the protection of the President.

Located in Washington, the United States Treasury Department is responsible for the printing and minting of currency and for the protection of the President.

Completeness
After *so, such, too*
Make your sentences complete in structure and thought, especially sentences with *so, such,* and *too.*

The house was so hot. (so hot that something must have happened)

The house was so hot that we had to turn on the air conditioner.

The room was in such confusion. (What happened?)

The room was in such confusion that we could not find the telephone book.

Omission of verbs and prepositions
Do not omit a verb or a preposition that is necessary to the structure of the sentence.

We were interested and then bored by the lecture.

We were interested in and then bored by the lecture.

The passengers were impatient and the plane late.

The passengers were impatient, and the plane was late.

Omission of *that*
The omission of *that* is often confusing.

INCOMPLETE

The museum said the painting was a forgery.

COMPLETE

The museum said that the painting was a forgery.

Comparisons

Make comparisons clear and complete by comparing only similar terms, using the word *other* where necessary, and avoiding awkward and incomplete comparisons.

INCORRECT

The bite of a great white shark is worse than a snake.

LOGICAL

The bite of a great white shark is worse than the bite of a snake.

INCORRECT

The Grand Canyon is larger than any canyon in the world.

LOGICAL

The Grand Canyon is larger than any other canyon in the world.

INCORRECT

Reading is one of the most pleasant if not the most pleasant pastime one can enjoy. (After *one of the most pleasant,* the plural *pastimes* is required.)

BETTER

Reading is one of the most pleasant pastimes one can enjoy, if not the most pleasant.

OR

Reading is one of the most pleasant pastimes.

Avoid ambiguous comparisons.

AMBIGUOUS

We enjoyed visiting the city more than our parents. (*More* than visiting parents, or *more* than the parents enjoyed the city?)

CLEAR

We enjoyed visiting the city more than our parents did.

Consistency

Avoid confusing shifts in grammatical forms.

Shifts in tense

The doctor was well trained, but his patients are dissatisfied.

The doctor is well trained, but his patients are dissatisfied.

Shifts in person

When we left our hotel, you could see the capitol building.

When we left our hotel, we could see the capitol building.

Shifts in number

A person may cheat on his income taxes, and then they deny it.

People cheat on their income taxes, and then they deny it.

Shifts in voice

The assignment *is read* by the student, and then she *answers* the questions at the end of the chapter. (Put both parts of the sentence in the active voice.)

The student *reads* the assignment, and then she *answers* the questions at the end of the chapter.

Excessive Coordination 8.1

Sentences should be varied in length, structure, and emphasis. Coordination, subordination, parallelism, and word order show relationships precisely and emphasize important elements of thought. Do not string together a number of short independent clauses; excessive coordination fails to show precise relationships between thoughts.

▶ *Rewrite the following sentences to eliminate excessive coordination.*

EXAMPLE

The election results are close and both candidates declared victory, so the officials decided to recount the ballots.

Because the election results were close and both candidates declared victory, the officials decided to recount the ballots.

1. The telephone rang, and the intercom buzzed, and his client walked in.

2. The engine started sluggishly, and the car ran badly, yet it recently had a tune-up.

3. Sales volume was up, but net profits decreased, for the rate of inflation had increased overhead.

_____

_____

_____

4. The performance was excellent, and actors and actresses thoroughly understood their roles, and so did the director.

_____

_____

_____

5. The operation started slowly, but it was a well-known franchise, and he had a good location.

_____

_____

_____

6. Cable television networks depend on revenues from advertisers, and they need payments from cable systems, yet commissions from telemarketing help as well.

_____

_____

_____

7. He never finished what he started, and seemed to try, and he devoted much time to each job.

_____

_____

_____

8. I could not eat the in-flight meal, and it was served during a heavy storm, and the plane dipped with each gust of wind.

_____

_____

_____

_____

9. He created an enclosed shopping village, and he divided an abandoned discount department store into 100 individual stores, and he paid utilities and maintenance, and each shopkeeper paid rent and advertising costs.

_____

_____

_____

_____

10. Real estate sales depend upon interest rates, and interest rates depend upon loan demand, and loan demand depends upon consumer confidence and governmental borrowing.

_____

_____

_____

_____

Subordination   8.2

▶ *Indicate which sentence in each of the following pairs is preferable because the writer either uses correct subordination or eliminates excessive coordination.*

EXAMPLE

___*a.*___ a. She wrote about conflict resolution, which centers on creating ways to resolve disputes.
b. She wrote about the field, which centers on creating ways to resolve disputes, of conflict resolution.

_____ 1. a. Because drive-in windows mean faster service, they bring business to fast-food chains.
b. Because they bring business to fast-food chains, drive-in windows mean faster service.

_____ 2. a. Although the postal service now offers electronic mail service, it hopes to attract more corporate customers.
b. The postal service, which now offers electronic mail service, hopes to attract more corporate customers.

_____ 3. a. Because robots can stand extremely high temperatures and can work at a fast pace, they have been designed to weld in ships' holds.
b. Robots have been designed to weld in the holds of ships, and they can stand extremely high temperatures and work at a fast pace.

_____ 4. a. The public prefers chain-link fencing, and cypress fencing is very durable.
b. Even though cypress is very durable, the public prefers chain-link fencing.

_____ 5. a. Carbon paper used to be an office mainstay, although it is now outdated.
b. Although carbon paper used to be an office mainstay, it is now outdated.

_____ 6. a. Some IRAs give the investor flexibility and professional management of retirement money while it accumulates.
b. While it accumulates, some IRAs give the investor flexibility and professional management of retirement money.

_____ 7. a. Most Americans have difficulty locating many of the new nations, but they are interested in foreign relations.

        b. Whereas most Americans have difficulty locating many of the new nations, they are interested in foreign relations.

_____ 8. a. Even though equipment and service are adequate, our company will improve both to meet new business requirements.

        b. Equipment is adequate, and service is also, and our company will continue to improve both to meet new business requirements.

_____ 9. a. Although public opinion polls have revealed Americans to be concerned about their environment, the environment is still polluted.

        b. Public opinion polls reveal Americans to be concerned about their environment, and the environment is still polluted.

_____ 10. a. Richard had little money to spare, but he bought a bouquet of flowers and surprised his date, and he was very thoughtful.

        b. Although he had little money to spare, Richard thoughtfully surprised his date with a bouquet of flowers.

Subordination   8.3

▶ *Revise the following sentences to achieve effective subordination.*

EXAMPLE

The last of our campaign funds were almost gone, and this caused the cancelation of most of the television advertisements.

When our campaign funds were almost gone, most of the television advertisements had to be canceled.

1. Foreign auto manufacturers now build cars in the United States, but some of them continue to import engines.

   _____

   _____

   _____

   _____

2. Component television was introduced in the United States in 1981, and it was introduced in Japan first.

   _____

   _____

   _____

   _____

3. You can buy a television monitor and a control, and these mean you can play video games and use your computer and watch a recorded tape and view regular programs and not disconnect one device to use another.

   _____

   _____

   _____

   _____

4. Barbara prefers older buildings which have windows that may be opened to allow breezes to circulate through the offices.

_____

_____

_____

5. Some airlines have a helicopter service from midtown to the airport, and it is free to first-class and business passengers.

_____

_____

_____

6. A Universal Product Code is a coded identification system placed on packaged food and other consumer items, and it can be read by an electronic scanner and transmits prices and other information to a cash register run by a computer.

_____

_____

_____

7. Systems analysts study businesses, and they first identify major goals, and they next develop procedures for the businesses to reach their goals.

_____

_____

_____

8. The electoral college is a group of electors who are chosen by voters in each state and who elect the president and who elect the vice president of the United States.

_____

_____

_____

9. A geographical area that surrounds a store or shopping center is a trading area and most of the retail trade is drawn from it.

_____

_____

_____

10. Copper is an element that is used for electrical wiring, and it once was used for plumbing; however, it now is too costly for plumbing.

_____

_____

_____

Completeness and Comparisons   8.4

▶ *Revise the following sentences to correct any errors in completeness and comparisons.*

EXAMPLES

The quota was too high.

The quota was too high to be a realistic incentive to the sales personnel.

Revising a report on a home computer is easier than any other way.

Revising a report on a home computer is easier than revising it any other way.

1. Telemarketing reaches more people.

   _____

   _____

2. The advertising campaign was as well run as if not better than any of the past.

   _____

   _____

3. The transit company is less profitable but more efficient.

   _____

   _____

4. The uncertain economic forecasts have and continue to disrupt the market.

   _____

   _____

5. Many people find a digital watch preferable.

   _____

   _____

6. A well-known brand name is as effective if not more so than a lower price.

_____

_____

7. Nonstop, coast-to-coast flights are as inexpensive if not more inexpensive today.

_____

_____

8. A good manager is both attentive and careful with details.

_____

_____

9. Four-cylinder engines may give better mileage, but they have less power.

_____

_____

10. The supervisor praised me more than the other buyer.

_____

_____

Completeness and Comparisons   8.5

▶ *Revise the following sentences to correct any errors in completeness and comparisons.*

EXAMPLE

No one works harder.

No one works harder than John.

1. A small business is better.

   _____

   _____

2. Their service is more reliable.

   _____

   _____

3. During January fewer consumers spend money.

   _____

   _____

4. Computers can be a more lucrative hobby.

   _____

   _____

5. Many pocket calculators are as inexpensive if not less expensive than five years ago.

   _____

   _____

6. The dean was both interested and concerned with the graduate's problems.

   _____

   _____

7. The new rules are as restrictive if not more restrictive as the ones in force ten years ago.

   _____

   _____

8. Poor timing is less easy to defend.

_____

_____

9. The jumbo jets have never and never will be able to land at our local airport.

_____

_____

10. Professional growth is both a reason and consequence of extensive reading in one's field.

_____

_____

Consistency 8.6

▶ *Revise the following sentences making them structurally consistent. Avoid unnecessary shifts in tense, person, mood, or voice and shifts from one relative pronoun to another.*

EXAMPLE

She was only thirty-two when she becomes the company's first woman president.

She was only thirty-two when she became the company's first woman president.

1. The work-flow is intermittent, since customer traffic was high only during certain hours of the day.

_____

_____

2. Everyone has a preference, and each had to compromise.

_____

3. The bank has worldwide resources and a fine reputation, which enabled it to raise large amounts of capital.

_____

4. The potholes had been repaired, and the crew then cleaned the streets.

_____

5. Because the competitor's prices were lower, they lower their own prices.

_____

6. One of the best tax lawyers was Linda Smith, who is my neighbor.

_____

_____

7. The buyers selected merchandise in the spring and wonder about the fall sales.

   _____

   _____

8. Publishers held their national convention in the spring and introduce new books.

   _____

   _____

9. Department stores plan advertising for Sunday, when presumably the paper was read more thoroughly.

   _____

   _____

10. If they are interested, they were attending the meeting.

    _____

    _____

Modifiers

Attach modifiers to the correct word or element in the sentence to avoid confusion. Most adjectives precede the noun they modify. Adverbs may come before or follow the words they modify. Prepositional phrases usually follow the word they modify, as do adjective clauses. Adverbial phrases and clauses may be placed in various positions—as decided by the writer.

EXAMPLES

The new tests are finished. (adjectives before the noun)

The new tests *soon* ended. (adverb before the verb)

The new tests ended *soon*. (adverb after the verb)

The man *on the corner* hailed a cab. (prepositional phrase modifying *man*)

The man came *to the door*. (prepositional phrase modifying *came*)

Sooner than we expected, the movie ended. (adverbial clause modifying *ended*)

The movie ended *sooner than we expected*. (adverbial clause modifying *ended*)

Dangling modifiers

Avoid dangling modifiers. A verbal phrase at the beginning of a sentence should modify the subject of the sentence.

Dangling participle

Seeing the fresh apple pie, *my hunger* grew.

CLEAR

Seeing the fresh apple pie, *I* grew hungry.

Dangling gerund

After examining my checkbook, *my error* was found.

CLEAR

After examining my checkbook, *I found* my error.

Dangling infinitive

To get an early start, *the alarm clock* was set for 6 A.M.

CLEAR

To get an early start, *I set* the alarm clock for 6 A.M.

Dangling prepositional phrase

While *in school*, my mother did her shopping.

CORRECT

While *I was* in school, my mother did her shopping.

Misplaced modifiers, squinting modifiers

Almost any modifier that comes between an adjective clause and the word it modifies can cause confusion.

UNCLEAR

Many people are released by the courts *who may be guilty*.

CLEAR

Many people *who may be guilty* are released by the courts.

A modifier placed between two words so that it may modify either word is a **squinting modifier.**

UNCLEAR

The chess master who was playing *carefully* won the first game.

CLEAR

The chess master who was *carefully* playing won the first game.

Separation of elements

Do not separate closely related elements, such as the subject and the verb, parts of a verb phrase, or a verb and an object.

AWKWARD

The construction workers *had,* for the last week, *expected* a new contract.

IMPROVED

For the last week, the construction workers *had expected* a new contract.

Avoid **split infinitives** (modifiers between *to* and the verb form).

NOT

to actively *pursue*

BUT

to pursue actively

Parallelism

Make construction in a sentence parallel (balanced) by matching phrase with phrase, clause with clause, verb with verb, and so on.

FAULTY

The men argued *bitterly* and *were loud*.

IMPROVED

The men argued *bitterly* and *loudly*.

Repeat an article *(a, an,* or *the),* a preposition *(by, in, for,* and so on), or other words to preserve parallelism and clarity.

FAULTY

The aircraft was *in a storm* and *trouble*.

IMPROVED

The aircraft was *in the storm* and *in trouble*.

Sentence variety

Vary sentences in structure and order. Use loose, periodic, and balanced sentence forms.

A **loose sentence** makes its main point at the beginning of the sentence and then adds qualifications or refinements.

We left early, missing the heavy traffic.

A **periodic sentence** saves the main point until the end of a sentence to create suspense or emphasis.

After a long afternoon visiting my aunt, I was eager to go home.

A **balanced sentence** has parallel parts in terms of structure, length, and thoughts.

We must work so that we may live, not live that we may work.

Position of Modifiers   9.1

▶ *Revise the following sentences to correct faulty modifiers.*

1. The buyer purchased the house with the most money.

   _____

   _____

2. We studied the new futures markets with great care.

   _____

   _____

3. Buying speculative stocks often made Ruth uneasy.

   _____

   _____

4. He told his customers after five o'clock that the store would be closed.

   _____

   _____

5. The discount broker is at the local mall that took my order to sell.

   _____

   _____

6. Spending money frequently causes problems.

   _____

   _____

7. Using a direct-mail campaign, our sales volume increased remarkably.

   _____

   _____

8. The universal life policy was recommended with guaranteed protection from inflation.

   _____

   _____

9. The Dow Jones Industrial Average gives greater weight to higher priced stocks, which is the oldest of the market indexes.

_____

_____

10. Trading in stock index futures is a way to hedge on overall market swings that is untested.

_____

_____

Position of Modifiers 9.2

▶ *Revise the following sentences to correct faulty modifiers.*

1. Reaching into the file, the bracelet dropped to the office floor.

   _____

   _____

2. Utilities benefit from a reduced inflation rate that have little short-term debt.

   _____

   _____

3. Plain-paper copiers with little space are cost-effective for small offices.

   _____

   _____

4. When starting a business, good advice on taxes is necessary.

   _____

   _____

5. To avoid unfavorable currency exchanges, a bank's advice should be sought.

   _____

   _____

6. The team could only draft one new player this year.

   _____

   _____

7. Driving west from Lordsburg, New Mexico, our sales meeting seemed far away.

   _____

   _____

8. Burrowing into the ground, I saw a badger near my cabin door.

   _____

   _____

9. By reinvesting profits, growth in the business became possible.

_____

_____

10. Looking for a discount coupon, lower list prices were ignored.

_____

_____

Separation of Elements 9.3

▶ *Do not unnecessarily separate closely related elements. Separation of parts of a verb phrase, a verb and its object, or a subject and its verb can be awkward or misleading. Revise the following sentences by correcting unnecessarily separated elements.*

EXAMPLE

New orders for household durables had, long before the second quarter, begun to increase.

New orders for household durables had begun to increase long before the second quarter.

1. The construction outlook improved, which had worsened last month, steadily.

   _____

   _____

2. Energy prices, after declining last year, increased.

   _____

   _____

3. Tod was overjoyed to receive, as a child would be, a pony for his birthday.

   _____

   _____

4. Ann, who managed the warehouse, was able to easily locate any item.

   _____

   _____

5. Be, when you are investing in commodities, very careful.

   _____

   _____

6. The cost of replacing our software was, although not as costly as feared, very high.

_____

_____

7. Although airline service was available in our town years ago, we now have regrettably only bus service.

_____

_____

8. We wanted to at least have one economic forecast that was not ambiguous.

_____

_____

9. The water had, to the consternation of us all, become too rough for sailing.

_____

_____

10. Several valuable trees, during the storm that struck the pecan groves, were uprooted.

_____

_____

Parallelism   9.4

▶ *Revise the following sentences to correct faulty parallelism.*

EXAMPLE
We invested with flair and profitably.

We invested with flair and profit.

1. Universal Life provides permanent protection, and that it gives flexible premiums is another feature.

   _____

   _____

2. The new vice president for finance spends much of her time studying the bond market and explains it to her staff members.

   _____

   _____

3. Sharon's favorite restaurant is noted for being quiet, convenient, and rarely has a large crowd.

   _____

   _____

4. Philip is an amiable insurance agent and who has a talent for golf.

   _____

   _____

5. The firm is seeking investment property that is near a shopping area, with a view of the sea, and with adequate parking.

   _____

   _____

6. City planners asked for help from an outside consultant, not only for his special technical knowledge, but he would be able to save the city money.

   _____

   _____

   _____

7. The market was rising all afternoon and rapidly excites the traders on Wall Street.

   _____

   _____

8. The counselor said that some young couples have difficulty following a budget, sharing problems, and with their children.

   _____

   _____

9. The flowers blossomed early and dazzling the visitors to the gardens.

   _____

   _____

10. The Special Olympics this year was helped by several civic organizations that obtained officials for each event, food for participants, and they had television coverage by local stations.

    _____

    _____

    _____

Parallelism 9.5

▶ *Revise the following sentences to correct faulty parallelism.*

EXAMPLE

The new diesel ran with a quiet tone and evenly.

The new diesel ran quietly and evenly.

1. Before I entered into business for myself, I had to see my attorney, contact my banker, and my broker found my small office.

   _____

   _____

2. Tanya taught advertising agents how to compile mailing lists, how to negotiate with the print media, and that maintaining good customer relations was important.

   _____

   _____

   _____

3. The law firm recruited a trial lawyer, estate planner, and a tax specialist interviewed.

   _____

   _____

4. Petroleum jobbers often own service stations, convenience stores, and other real estate is their secondary business.

   _____

   _____

5. Following the regional meeting, the sales representatives conferred briefly, and routine assignments awaited.

   _____

   _____

6. He likes to swim, to jog, and weightlifting.

   _____

   _____

7. The new financial strategy is a combination of borrowing from commercial banks, attracting private investors, and to use internally generated capital.

_____

_____

_____

8. Fashion models need make-up artists, good agents, and common sense should help.

_____

_____

9. He asked Mary if she had sold her quota, and wasn't he surprised at her answer.

_____

_____

10. Accountants need to know mathematics, tax law, and a working knowledge of computers helps.

_____

_____

Variety in Sentences 9.6

▶ *Make one sentence out of each of the groups below. Vary your sentences in length, structure, and order. Write simple, compound, and complex patterns, and vary your sentences between loose, periodic, and balanced forms. A loose sentence, the most frequent kind, makes the main point early and then adds refinements. A periodic sentence withholds an element of the main thought until the end and thus creates suspense and emphasis. A balanced sentence has parts which are similar in structure and length and which express parallel thoughts.*

EXAMPLE

A corporate manager must know business law.
A company is liable for actions of employees.
It even is liable if employees disobey policy.

A corporate manager must know business law because his company is liable for the actions of employees, even those who disobey policy.

1. Albert is the local appliance dealer.
    Our dishwasher was broken.
    We had it repaired on Thursday.

    _____

    _____

    _____

    _____

2. Several theaters in New York City may be torn down.
    The Helen Hayes Theater is one of them.
    Builders plan to construct hotels and convention facilities.

    _____

    _____

    _____

    _____

3. Some word processors do more than print.
   They actually proofread original copies.
   The first copies therefore are letter-perfect.

   _____

   _____

   _____

   _____

   _____

4. There is a restaurant on the top floor of The Bank of America Building.
   This building is in San Francisco.
   Diners can view the entire bay area from there.

   _____

   _____

   _____

   _____

   _____

5. Electronic printing systems are efficient.
   They translate computerized data into print.
   Some print graphics as well.

   _____

   _____

   _____

   _____

   _____

6. Laser technology has modernized the business office.
   It allows computerized printers to merge graphics with texts.
   Costs for price lists, manuals, and catalogs are thus cut.

   _____

   _____

   _____

   _____

   _____

7. Corporations may raise money abroad at cheaper rates.
   European and Middle Eastern lenders trust American corporations.
   Often they avoid taxes in their own countries.

   _____

   _____

   _____

8. Corporate officers are paid to make decisions.
   They must make hard, often expensive ones.
   They need accurate data.

   _____

   _____

   _____

9. The store opened an hour early.
   The sale was the biggest in years.
   The shoppers rushed in.

   _____

   _____

   _____

10. Start-up costs for new ventures must be controlled carefully.
    Investing in new ideas becomes less of a gamble.
    Losses are limited and do not affect overall earnings.

    _____

    _____

    _____

138

Variety in Sentences   9.7

▶ *Revise the following sentences for greatest emphasis and for the most logical or climactic order. Write C to the left of any correct sentence.*

EXAMPLE

On the legislative agenda are tax reform, billboard regulations, and new committee assignments.

On the legislative agenda are new committee assignments, billboard regulations, and tax reform.

(Revised to move from least to most important item.)

1. The order came through when we expressed our concern.

_____

_____

_____

_____

2. Convention guests danced until midnight, ate dinner, and were greeted by their hosts.

_____

_____

_____

_____

3. Good interviews cause many people to get jobs and give them much anxiety.

_____

_____

_____

_____

4. The news upset an entire segment of the market, interrupted routine business, and damaged the government's ties with Wall Street.

_____

_____

_____

5. The modern dentist needs a licensed dental assistant, a good bookkeeper, and state-of-the-art equipment.

_____

_____

_____

6. Mr. Robertson, our neighbor, has been a lieutenant colonel in the army, a senator in Washington, and a member of the local school board.

_____

_____

_____

7. A physician's assistant must have formal training, a good rapport with others, and a thorough internship.

_____

_____

_____

8. The chef asked each of the kitchen workers who had caused the meat to spoil and left the freezer door open.

_____

_____

_____

9. Wally's boss was so angry because part of the office staff was late again that he threw his briefcase on his desk, threatened to fire everyone, and demanded to know why they were late.

_____

_____

_____

10. A good business letter reveals factual knowledge, a calm demeanor, and clear thinking.

   _____

   _____

   _____

Copyright © 1983 by Houghton Mifflin Company

Variety in Sentences 9.8

▶ *Identify the following sentences as loose or periodic.*

EXAMPLE

After many weeks of problems, the business improved. *periodic*

The business improved after many weeks of problems. *loose*

1. The crowd lining the street began to applaud when the president's car approached. _____

2. Because we had had no rain for several weeks, one local man said it was so dry that the water in his well tasted dusty. _____

3. Because interest rates were so reasonable, we decided to borrow money to finance new inventory. _____

4. Although most people believe that sports franchises are lucrative, many are really tax write-offs. _____

5. Calculators can make mistakes, even though people trust the computations to be accurate. _____

6. Some scientists think a chemical in mushrooms, garlic, and onions may reduce the chances of developing cancer when these vegetables are eaten on a regular basis. _____

7. Only practical experience, academic training, and relevant personal data should be on a résumé, however much we would like to include other questionable items. _____

8. Personality, self-confidence, and enthusiasm count most in an interview, although neatness speaks volumes, too. _____

9. Because job interviews are very important, candidates should prepare themselves well. _____

10. We helped computerize the warehouse records by
    arranging for a competent consultant.   _____

Variety in Sentences   9.9

▶ *Make the following loose sentences into periodic ones.*

EXAMPLE

The chief operating officer is a necessary position, because committees cannot run the daily operations of a company.

Because committees cannot run the daily operations of a company, the chief operating officer is a necessary position.

1. The industrial exhibition was a tremendous success because the planning committee had contacted dozens of manufacturers.

   _____

   _____

2. We visited the World's Fair in Knoxville while we were vacationing in Tennessee.

   _____

   _____

3. The labor contract was signed in less than a week, although neither party to the negotiations had expected a quick agreement.

   _____

   _____

4. In the near future microchips in computers will store hundreds of times as much information as they do now if the predictions of engineers and scientists are correct.

   _____

   _____

5. We were especially impressed by our guide's knowledge of the history of the movie studio while we were on our tour.

   _____

   _____

6. A limited partnership must have a least two partners in most states.

   _____

   _____

7. About 70 percent of the television sets sold in the United States are made in Japan if the latest statistics are accurate.

   _____

   _____

8. Public announcements of presidential orders and proclamations must appear in the *Federal Register* before they become effective.

   _____

   _____

9. The Rogun Dam in Russia will be 1,250 feet high when it is completed.

   _____

   _____

10. Throughout history men have envied birds because they can fly.

    _____

    _____

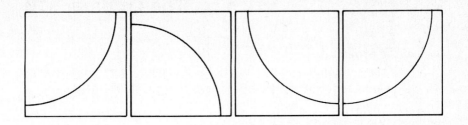

Punctuation

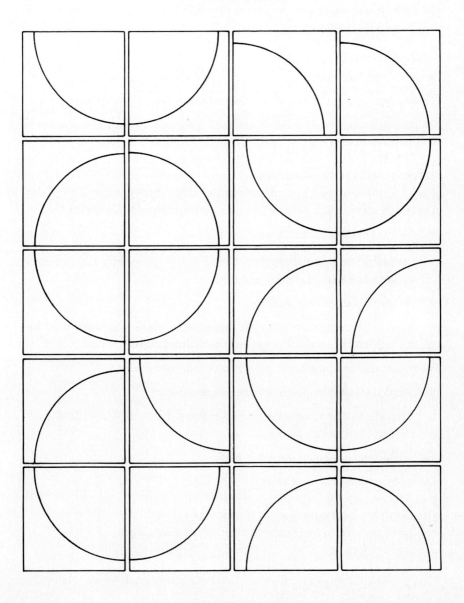

Uses of the comma
Although the comma has many functions, it is used, in general, to separate elements and to set off modifiers or parenthetical elements.

Between two independent clauses
Use the comma to separate independent clauses joined by a coordinating conjunction *(and, but, or, nor, for, so, yet)*.

The brisk winds raised only moderate waves, *but* the falling barometer indicated stormy weather was coming.

In a series
Use a comma between words, phrases, and clauses in a series.

We chose red, gold, and white for our color scheme. (words in a series)

The audience was seated, the overture had begun, and the curtain was about to open. (clauses in a series)

Between coordinate adjectives
Use a comma between **coordinate adjectives** not joined by *and*. Coordinate adjectives each modify the noun (or pronoun) independently.

The *gloomy, uninhabited* house was very isolated.

Cumulative adjectives do not modify independently. Do not use a comma between cumulative adjectives.

He discarded his *shabby old* clothes.

Note: to recognize coordinate adjectives, place the word *and* between them and determine whether they sound right.

The gloomy *and* uninhabited house was isolated. (sounds right)

He discarded his shabby *and* old clothes. (sounds wrong)

Another test is to reverse the adjectives. Normally, coordinate adjectives are easily reversible.

uninhabited, gloomy house (sounds right)

old shabby clothes (sounds wrong)

After long introductory clauses or phrases
Use a comma after a long introductory phrase or clause.

At the end of my first full day at work, I was ready for a good dinner. (phrase)

When my first full day at work ended, I was ready for a good dinner. (clause)

Introductory verbal phrases usually are set off by a comma.

Working alone, she built a new room at the mountain retreat. (participial phrase)

To prepare for the race, the runner trained for weeks. (infinitive phrase)

After finishing dinner, we took a long walk. (prepositional phrase)

With nonrestrictive elements
Use commas to set off nonrestrictive appositives, phrases, and clauses that add description or information but are not essential to the meaning of the sentence.

Mary Evans, *the company comptroller,* was invited to a meeting in Washington. (nonrestrictive appositive phrase)

Mary Evans, *who is the company comptroller,* was invited to a meeting in Washington. (nonrestrictive adjective clause)

Note that a restrictive element is *never* set off by commas, since it is necessary for the meaning of the total sentence.

The music *that we most enjoy* is contemporary.

With parenthetical elements
Use commas with parenthetical elements.

We are prepared to continue the project, *we believe,* if there is enough public interest.

With conjunctive adverbs
Use a comma after a conjunctive adverb (*however, nevertheless, moreover, furthermore,* and so on) when it precedes an independent clause.

The profit margin was down; *however,* next year should be better.

With unusual word order
Use commas with sentence elements out of normal word order.

The cowboy, *haggard and thin,* slowly saddled his horse.

With degrees, titles, dates, places, addresses
Use commas with degrees and titles, as well as to separate elements in dates, places, and addresses.

Rosa Adams, M.D., joined the staff. (comma before and after *M.D.*)

On March 10, 1971, my daughter was born. (comma before and after year)

On Monday, December 19, the Christmas vacation begins.

BUT

In July 1969 we bought a new home. (optional commas)

The year 1945 marked the end of World War II. (no comma)

Sedona, Arizona, is at the entrance to Oak Creek Canyon. (Use a comma before and after the name of a state.)

My new address is 196 Warner Avenue, Westwood, California 73520. (no comma before zip code)

For contrast or emphasis
Use commas for contrast and emphasis as well as for short interrogative elements.

I want the new price list, not this one.

The dog stood still, not moving a muscle.

I was correct, wasn't I?

With mild interjections and *yes* or *no*
Use commas with mild interjections and with words like *yes* and *no*.

Well, I was almost right.

Yes, we agree to your offer.

With direct address
Use commas with words in direct address.

"Roberta, I need your help."

Use commas with expressions like *he said* or *she replied* when used with quoted matter.

"I cannot find my raincoat," *he complained*.

With absolute phrases
Set off an **absolute phrase** with a comma. An absolute phrase, which consists of a noun followed by a modifier, modifies an entire sentence.

The restaurant being closed, we decided to go home.

To prevent misreading or to mark an omission
Use commas to prevent misreading or to mark an omission.

Above, the wind howled through the trees.

The summer days were hot and dry; the night, warm and humid. (comma for omitted verb *was*)

Unnecessary commas

Between subject and verb
Do not use a comma between subject and verb, between verb or verbal and complement, or between an adjective and the word it modifies.

The team with the best record, will go to the playoffs.

We saw, that the window had been left open.

The shining wrapping, paper got one's attention.

Between compound elements
Do not use a comma between compound elements, such as verbs, subjects, complements, and predicates.

We went to the local library, and perused *The New York Times*. (compound verb; comma unnecessary)

Between dependent clauses
Do not use a comma before a coordinating conjunction joining two dependent clauses.

We checked to see that the lights were off, and that all the doors were locked. (comma unnecessary)

In comparisons
Do not use a comma before *than* in a comparison or between compound conjunctions such as *as . . . as, so . . . so, so . . . that*.

The electrician found more wrong with the washing machine, than we had expected.

It was so hot, that the engine overheated.

After *like, such as*
Do not use a comma after *like* or *such as*.

Many famous paintings such as, the *Mona Lisa* and *View of Toledo* are almost priceless.

A comma is used before *such as* only when the phrase is nonrestrictive.

Do not use a comma directly before or after a period, a question mark, an exclamation point, or a dash.

NOT

"Were you late for work?", he asked.

With parentheses

A comma may follow a closing parenthesis but may not come before an opening parenthesis.

After reading *A Tale of Two Cities* (written by Charles Dickens), one understands the complexity of the French Revolution.

Other unnecessary commas

Do not use commas after coordinating conjunctions.

NOT

We did not like the accommodations at the hotel, but, we found nothing else available. (Retain comma before *but;* delete comma after *but*.)

A comma is not required after short adverbial modifiers.

After a rain the desert blooms with wildflowers. (no comma required after *rain*)

Do not use commas to set off restrictive clauses, phrases, or appositives.

NOT

The water level, *at the lake,* is low. (restrictive prepositional phrase)

Do not use a comma between adjectives that are cumulative and not coordinate. (See p. 148.)

FAULTY

The new, Persian rug was beautiful.

The Comma with Independent Clauses   10.1

▶ *In the following sentences, insert and encircle commas between independent clauses. In the blank at the right, enter the comma and the coordinating conjunction. If a sentence is correct, write* C.

EXAMPLE

The company provides a series of seminars for those who like to keep abreast of information sources⊙ and they also specialize in uncovering sources from the federal government.

,and

1. Mailing lists are an essential advertising tool and they are available in great variety. _____

2. The *Wall Street Journal* is a respected newspaper for it reports general news stories in addition to business news. _____

3. Manufacturers of satellite dishes expect their industry to grow, and they cite the growth figures of cable television stations, which buy their products, as evidence. _____

4. Pecan shells have some commercial value, for they are used to make glue for plywood. _____

5. The prices of antiques vary from region to region and they also fluctuate with the inflation rate. _____

6. The company has toll-free hotlines and it receives several calls a day. _____

7. This portable computer sells for under $2,000.00 but its competing model sells for almost $4,000.00. _____

8. This whistle blew at 5:00 P.M. and the workers left for their homes. _____

9. Metal shelves come in several colors but are not as sturdy as oak shelves. _____

10. I attended the firm's workshop on annuities but I could
    not attend the reception. _____

The Comma with Independent Clauses   10.2

▶ *In the following sentences, insert and encircle commas between independent clauses. In the blank at the right, enter the comma and the coordinating conjunction. If a sentence is correct, write* C.

1. Domestic consumption of coal will set new records and coal mining has become a growth industry. _____

2. Some brokers use mailing lists to make contacts, but often they get a disappointing response. _____

3. The financial futures market was laughed at ten years ago but it is booming now. _____

4. Cooperative advertising saves money, and it usually guarantees higher sales. _____

5. Bills of lading should be checked carefully and they must be filed immediately. _____

6. The new mall needed an anchor store but the developers could not find one with good recognition. _____

7. Many supermarkets now carry nonfood items and this practice is known as scrambled merchandising. _____

8. Most banks offer their best customers lines of credit, for this policy streamlines business operations. _____

9. New ventures need adequate working capital, and good consultants help them compute exact needs. _____

10. The modern cash register is also a computer terminal for with electronic scanners it tabulates sales and takes inventory simultaneously. _____

The Comma with Items in Series   10.3

▶ *Insert commas as necessary in items in series.*

EXAMPLE

Four necessary periodicals for today's investor are the *Wall Street Journal*, *Business Week*, *Forbes*, and *Barrons*.

1. Charities depend on individuals churches and corporations.

2. Prices for metals timber and textiles eventually will rise.

3. She invested in utilities electronics and cosmetics.

4. The physical appearance of a store should be bright clean and inviting.

5. A consumer's decision to purchase a product is based on brand cost and need.

6. Consumerism hopes to guarantee safety quality and truth in the marketplace.

7. Many birds help control insect rodent and reptile populations.

8. Feed grains dairy products and winter wheat are exported by the United States.

9. They decided to attend the luncheon to shop and then to return to the hotel.

10. Retailers often shop one another's outlets to investigate prices inventories and promotions.

The Comma with Coordinate Adjectives   10.4

▶ *Insert commas as necessary between coordinate adjectives.*

EXAMPLE
Large chain stores need spacious, attractive entrances.

1. Colorful broad prints characterized the new fashions.

2. Merchandising for new products includes mailing small inexpensive samples.

3. Detailed graphic illustrations marked the annual report.

4. Accessible time-saving locations are necessary for so-called convenience stores.

5. Regulated common carriers must maintain regular established routes.

6. Some suppliers offer discounts to credit-worthy large-volume buyers.

7. Costly uncontrollable overhead can cut profits quickly.

8. A timely inexpensive loss leader can attract consumer traffic.

9. An interesting imaginative shopping environment does not have to be expensive.

10. Accurate reliable market research need not suppress creativity.

NAME _____

DATE _____ SCORE _____

The Comma After Introductory Clauses or Phrases 10.5

▶ *Place commas as needed after introductory clauses or phrases. In the space at the right, place the comma and write the word after it. If no comma is necessary in any sentence, write C.*

EXAMPLE

Because the administration wanted to stimulate the econ-

omy₍?₎it recommended a tax rebate.   _____,it_____

1. Although most agree that a good climate for business is important few define the elusive term.   _____

2. During the last two decades population—and hence manufacturing—has shifted to the Sunbelt.   _____

3. If state governments have a future role in industrial expansion it will be to provide technical training.   _____

4. What one says is surely as important as how one speaks.   _____

5. In the article the secretary of commerce predicts future export trends.   _____

6. Whatever goes down the pipe must be filtered.   _____

7. After a city's tax base shrinks it may lose its good bond rating.   _____

8. Because the cost of land and construction is high textile manufacturers hesitate to expand.   _____

9. When I installed a long-range antenna I improved the short-wave reception.   _____

10. Interested more in an abundant unskilled labor supply apparel firms generally train their own workers.   _____

The Comma After Introductory Clauses or Phrases 10.6

▶ *Place commas as needed after introductory clauses or phrases. In the space provided at the right, place the comma and write the word after it. If no comma is necessary in any sentence, write* C.

1. When a company decides on a new location it strongly considers good transportation and proximity to markets. _____

2. Unlike apparel firms furniture manufacturers search for skilled labor. _____

3. For the chemical industry environmental regulations are of the utmost importance. _____

4. After we made a survey we found that new facilities usually are branches of out-of-state corporations. _____

5. Over the past few years the Pacific region has had large increases in manufacturing. _____

6. While tax incentives may attract some industry regions seeking it should stress their large markets. _____

7. Refusing to purchase new computerized looms the weaver preferred to design products manually. _____

8. While most lumber comes from softwood much furniture comes from hardwoods such as oak. _____

9. Because mortgage rates rose quite high realtors looked for alternatives to conventional financing. _____

10. In the 1940s big dance bands were very popular. _____

The Comma with Nonrestrictive Elements   10.7

▶ *Correctly punctuate nonrestrictive elements in the following sentences. Write C to the right of any correctly punctuated sentence. Circle punctuation that you add.*

EXAMPLE

Recently the South(,)much like the North and the West earlier this century(,) has become the recipient of migration.   _____

1. The policy being written for our workers is excellent.   _____

2. The package that I sent to California last week still has not arrived.   _____

3. The architect an outspoken critic of anything modern believed in traditional designs.   _____

4. A noncredit plan that has some similarities to revolving credit plans is the layaway system.   _____

5. The bank president who was our annual speaker discussed monetary policy.   _____

6. An order that is sent to a vendor for merchandise not regularly stocked is called a special order.   _____

7. The display window filled with moving marionettes attracted the attention of Christmas shoppers.   _____

8. The ship with its cargo intact sailed into port for repairs.   _____

9. Wall Street which indeed once ran alongside a wall is the site of the New York Stock Exchange.   _____

10. Public accountants who must pass state examinations spend years both in formal training and internships.   _____

The Comma—All Uses 10.8

▶ *Correctly punctuate the following sentences. Circle punctuation that you add.*

EXAMPLE

Denver, Colorado, and Atlanta, Georgia, are two of the most rapidly growing cities in the United States.

1. Dates for organizational meetings are December 10 1983 and February 4 1984.

2. Janice M. Alden C.L.U. is now a partner with Smith Jones and Kent.

3. Consumers with complaints may write the Federal Trade Commission Washington D.C.

4. All new structures—the library the administration building and the maintenance plant—are energy efficient.

5. The DeLorean an automobile made of stainless steel was manufactured in Northern Ireland.

6. Although the price of wheat is down it will increase as the export market expands.

7. Houghton Mifflin Company located at One Beacon Street Boston Massachusetts 02107 is a major publisher of textbooks.

8. This manual is designed to teach the basic languages of the computer to teach the programming of a desk computer and to acquaint the customer with other models.

9. As pension funds retreat from real estate they may be missing some good buys.

10. Judge Dale a graduate of the University of Texas Law School was named to the panel of jurists.

The Comma—All Uses 10.9

▶ *Correctly punctuate the following sentences. Circle punctuation that you add.*
  Write C in the blank at the right if the sentence is correct.

1. Elise McFarland editor-in-chief of *Outdoor Advertising*
   wrote of the value of scientific marketing.   _____

2. Citizens of our city often travel fifty miles to shop in Dallas.   _____

3. The consumer who wrote the letter included a copy of the
   limited warranty.   _____

4. The key to good investment which I only recently have
   discovered is to avoid following the crowd.   _____

5. Even though many speculative stocks pay small divi-
   dends their potential for growth is impressive.   _____

6. Because I heard the telephone ringing I hurried into the
   office.   _____

7. Major credit cards once distributed free of charge now
   cost fifteen dollars annually.   _____

8. While the eight-track tape system had a better sound I
   preferred the more convenient cassette recorder.   _____

9. Having faith in the experiment accounted for the scientists' success.   _____

10. Whereas many mutual funds are perhaps overdiversi-
    fied their investment goals continue to require prudent
    diversification.   _____

Unnecessary Commas   10.10

▶ *Circle all unnecessary commas in the following sentences.*

EXAMPLE

A stockholder(,)who never votes(,)should not criticize elected directors.

1. The research division, ranked farm-credit securities, very high.

2. A bold, countermove by the board of directors discouraged would-be takeovers.

3. The veteran, financial officer, calm and patient, directed all securities transactions.

4. No one seemed to notice, our arriving, somewhat, late, to the board meeting.

5. Land-use studies are a, necessary, ingredient, for good, public planning.

6. Currency traders much have, knowledge, flexibility, and good nerves.

7. The new, green drapes, added to our office's serene atmosphere.

8. The supervisor, who is my uncle, encouraged me to continue working, with the company, while I attended school.

9. A pediatrician, with a specialty in allergies, usually, attracts many patients.

10. An effective prospectus, is a document, organized for potential customers who may not be specialists.

Unnecessary Commas 10.11

▶ *Circle all unnecessary commas in the following sentences.*

EXAMPLE

Jones ⊙ and Smith were promoted earlier than expected.

1. Managed forests, are a necessity for companies in the wood-products business.

2. Financial staffs, of many corporations, are becoming more independent of banks.

3. The insurance industry is undergoing a rapid, yet, significant evolution.

4. Large, institutional investors, such as mutual funds, usually hire a team of professional, money managers.

5. Efficient, water management is crucial economically in some, arid western states.

6. The state, of Connecticut, has no income tax and, hence, attracts many, high-income citizens.

7. Individual, Retirement Accounts, called IRAs, are most popular with middle-aged people.

8. Fashions change, from year to year, and often styles return, years after they disappeared.

9. Passenger trains are very popular, in Europe and Japan, where there are few highways, like the interstate systems of the United States.

10. The price of gold usually rises during times of global, political crisis, and falls rapidly thereafter.

The semicolon

Between two independent clauses
Use a semicolon between independent clauses not joined by *and, but, or, nor, for, so, yet.*

We hiked to the top of the mountain; we looked out over a valley covered with wildflowers.

Use a semicolon with a conjunctive adverb when it is followed by an independent clause.

We stayed until late afternoon; then we made our way back to camp.

Use a semicolon to separate independent clauses that are long and complex or that have internal punctuation.

Central City, located near Denver, was once a mining town; but now it is noted for its summer opera program.

Between items in a series
Use semicolons in a series between items that have internal punctuation.

In his closet Bill kept a photograph album, which was empty; several tennis shoes, all with holes in them; and the radiator cap from his first car, which he sold his first year in college.

Do not use a semicolon between elements that are not coordinate.

INCORRECT
After publishing *The Day of the Jackal* and several other popular novels; Frederick Forsyth wrote his most exciting book, *The Devil's Alternative*. (Use a comma, not a semicolon.)

The colon
Use the colon before quotations, statements, and series that are introduced formally.

The geologist began his speech with a disturbing statement: "This country is short of rare metals."

Use a colon to introduce a formal series.

Bring the following items: food for a week, warm clothes, bedding, and a canteen.

Between two independent clauses
Use a colon between two independent clauses when the second explains the first.

The team's record was excellent: we have not lost a game this season.

For special uses
Use the colon between hours and minutes.

4:35 P.M.

Unnecessary colon
Do not use a colon *after* a linking verb or a preposition.

INCORRECT
Our representatives are: Anne Crane and Andrew Miles.

He was accustomed to: hard work, good pay, and long weekends.

The dash
Use the dash to introduce summaries or to show interruption, parenthetical comment, or special emphasis.

For summary
Clothing, blankets, food, medicine—anything will help.

For interruption
"I want to say how sad—I mean happy—I am to be here," the speaker stumbled.

For parenthetical comments
This is important—I mean really important—so listen carefully.

For special emphasis
The key to the mystery could only be in one place—the attic.

Parentheses
Use parentheses to enclose loosely related comments or explanations or to enclose numbers used to indicate items in a series.

That year (1950) was the happiest time of my life.

Please do the following: (1) fill out the form, (2) include a check or money order, and (3) list any special mailing instructions.

Brackets
Use brackets to enclose *interpolations,* that is, the writer's explanations, within a passage that is being quoted.

The senator objected, "I cannot agree with your [Senator Miner's] reasoning." (brackets used to set off writer's interpolation)

The Semicolon 11.1

▶ *Insert semicolons where they are needed in the following sentences. If necessary, cross out other marks of punctuation. Circle semicolons that you add.*

EXAMPLE
Economics was once known as the dismal science (;) now it is a very popular field.

1. Many people enjoy starting new businesses they are called entrepreneurs.

2. Every corporation must have a president, a secretary and a treasurer, the latter two offices may be combined.

3. Recent surveys show that citizens are worried about unemployment their second concern is food costs.

4. Most large banks have trust departments, many medium-sized banks are seeking trust accounts, too.

5. In recent years many have begun to take interest in personal health as a result, books discussing preventive medicine have sold thousands of copies.

6. Real estate developers should review zoning regulations, these regulations can determine property values.

7. Few people would enjoy eating insects, however, in terms of protein locusts, spiders, and termites contain more than twice as much as chicken or beef.

8. A single swarm of locusts in East Africa can cover over 608 square miles, in terms of food value this translates into over 100,000 tons of edible protein.

9. That we cannot regulate large economies is evident underground economies thrive in government-controlled systems.

10. The Space Shuttle's remote manipulator arm can lift thirty-two tons in space on earth it cannot lift itself.

The Semicolon   11.2

▶ *Insert semicolons where they are needed in the following sentences. If necessary, cross out other marks of punctuation. Circle semicolons that you add.*

EXAMPLE
The work was strenuous; in fact, the workers were exhausted.

1. Discount brokerages are not new they are now thriving, however.

2. Housing costs have soared in the last decade modular home sales have soared as well.

3. The fishing industry depends on clean water it also needs dependable markets.

4. Metal automobile bodies may be a thing of the past in the next decade carbon fibers made from coal may replace metal.

5. Light actually has weight of a sort sunlight on the earth's surface exerts a pressure of about two pounds per square mile.

6. Tourism depends on a healthy economy, people do not spend discretionary money on vacations during recessions.

7. A strong dollar usually means fewer exports, however, a very weak dollar may indicate worldwide inflation.

8. Glass is composed of some of the most common substances on earth however, it once was considered to be so precious that only the nobility could own it.

9. Sand that is used to remove paint and corrosion from buildings often enters the lungs of workers some scientists believe that dry ice would be just as effective as sand and much safer.

10. Newspapers frequently carry stories about oil spills in the world's oceans, however, rainstorm runoffs from neighborhoods, industries, and highways may cause more near-shore damage to the environment than oil-tanker disasters.

Colons and Dashes   11.3

▶ *Correctly punctuate the following sentences. Circle punctuation that you add.*
Write C to the left of any sentence that is correct.

EXAMPLE
All of New England—Connecticut, Maine, Massachusetts, New Hampshire,
Rhode Island, and Vermont—is likely to suffer serious fuel shortages during
bad winters.

1. Fifty years from now, nearly 20 percent of all Americans about 65
   million people will be sixty-five years old or older.

2. At 7 30 this morning the contract expired, but a strike is unlikely.

3. The development of many new products is hindered by but a single
   problem cost.

4. One reason that construction costs increase with petroleum prices
   is simple asphalt is made with petroleum.

5. Hundreds of conventional blue-collar jobs electrical contracting,
   bus driving, building maintenance are open to women.

6. The professions medicine, law, pharmacy, accounting also are open
   to women.

7. The chief judgment one makes in an interview is subjective does
   the candidate have the right personality?

8. The office bulletin board had only one announcement "This office
   will be closed July 4."

9. Our firm needs skilled help in three areas statistics, programming,
   and personnel.

10. All of us Ted, Rachel, Meg, and me joined the same professional associations.

Parentheses and Brackets   11.4

▶ *Insert parentheses and brackets where they are needed in the following sentences. Circle parentheses and brackets that you add.*

EXAMPLE
The insurance policy (purchased in 1950) has a sizable cash value.

1. Please provide the following information: 1 professional experience, 2 special skills, 3 academic training.

2. President John F. Kennedy 1960–1963 was a strong supporter of our space program.

3. "I did not see it the signal light, officer," the driver protested.

4. The highest salaries averaging about $32,000.00 are offered to new graduates of the best law schools.

5. The year 1965 this firm was founded, the market was healthy, and the commissions were high.

6. Follow the arrows on the wall to find the department you need: the top arrow yellow leads to the executive offices, the middle arrow blue leads to research and development, and the bottom arrow black leads to shipping.

7. At that time 11:30 A.M. the formal announcement of the merger will be issued to the press.

8. His motion pictures there were 20 were never popular with the public but were acclaimed by the critics.

9. Howard McKey pronounced McKay is our new company representative in New York City.

10. Before making your payment, make certain that you have 1 signed your check, 2 enclosed a copy of the bill with your check, and 3 placed a stamp on the envelope.

Quotation Marks and End Punctuation 12

Quotation marks
Use quotation marks to enclose the exact words of a speaker or writer.

"I'm tired," he said. (declarative statement and object of verb *said*)

"Come here," she demanded. (command)

"Who's ready to leave?" Mary asked. (question)

"Quick!" he shouted. (exclamation)

Periods and *commas* always are placed inside quotation marks. *Semicolons* and *colons* always are placed outside quotation marks. *Question marks* and *exclamation points* are placed inside quotation marks when they refer to the quotation itself. They are placed outside the quotation marks when they refer to the entire sentence.

Who said, "We need a new car"? (Quotation is a statement.)

Use quotation marks to enclose dialogue. Do not use quotation marks with indirect quotation.

Alexander Pope once wrote, "A little learning is a dangerous thing." (direct quotation)

Alexander Pope said that a little learning can be dangerous. (indirect quotation)

In dialogue a new paragraph marks each change of speaker.

"Do you have change for a dollar?" the customer asked, after searching in his pocket for change.
"I think so," replied the cashier.

Quotation within a quotation
Use single quotation marks to enclose a quotation within a quotation.

John complained, "I don't understand your comment, 'Be clear first, then clever.' "

Titles
Use quotation marks to enclose the titles of essays, articles, short stories, chapters, television programs, and short musical compositions.

We enjoy reading William Safire's column, "On Language," in the Sunday newspaper. (article in newspaper)

Many people do not know whether to like or to hate the CBS program "60 Minutes." (television program)

The band began to play Sousa's "Stars and Stripes Forever." (musical composition)

Unnecessary quotations

Do not use quotation marks to emphasize or change the usual meanings of words or to point out the use of slang or attempts at humor.

NOT

We had a "great" time at the party. (emphasis)

That movie was really "bad." (change of meaning)

I guess we "goofed." (slang)

His lemonades are so bad that they always turn out to be "lemons." (attempted humor)

End punctuation

Use a **period** after sentences that make statements and after sentences that express command which is not exclamatory.

The humidity made us uncomfortable. (statement)

Meet us after the concert. (mild command)

Use a **question mark** after a direct question.

What time is it?

Use an **exclamation point** after a word, a phrase, or a sentence to indicate strong feeling.

Ouch! That hurt!

Stop that man!

Remember to use a period after mild exclamations.

That is the craziest idea I ever heard.

Quotation Marks and End Punctuation   12.1

▶ *Correctly punctuate the following sentences. Circle any incorrect punctuation and indicate what punctuation should be used. Indicate a new paragraph with the sign ¶.*

EXAMPLE

"What kinds of bonds are those⊙" asked the intern. "Municipal," replied the broker.

1. Please call your secretary, read the message.

2. Oh! exclaimed my partner, Our stock went up!

3. You must vent all wood stoves, warned the sales representative.

4. How can I be certain of these price quotations, inquired the cautious buyer.

5. The advertisement stated the counsel's opinion: We find the bond sale to be legal.

6. To relieve jet lag, said the flight attendant, try to rest one hour in the hotel room.

7. A good warranty is worth a higher price, advised the clerk.

8. The letter unequivocally stated: Management recommends an affirmative vote on the proposed new directors.

9. We are very proud of all contestants, reiterated the master of ceremonies.

10. Shall I telephone our supplier asked the clerk. I think not, replied the manager. We have more merchandise on the floor.

Quotation Marks and End Punctuation   12.2

▶ *Correctly punctuate the following sentences. Circle any incorrect punctuation.*
Indicate a new paragraph with the sign¶.

EXAMPLE
"Help! I need more lead time," said the vendor.

1. Up! Climb higher! shouted the spectators.

2. The gum tree grows in swampy terrain, said the forester. Early settlers used its bark to clean their teeth.

3. The auctioneer shouted: Sold for $1,000.00.

4. The pilot informed us: We are now over the Rocky Mountains and will land in one hour.

5. The underwriter told his bankers: I need your support with this new stock issue.

6. How must we heat this new plant the engineer wondered aloud.

7. The stockbroker asked: How do you intend to beat inflation over the next few years?

8. Consumer prices declined during the first quarter; however, unemployment rose slightly, reported the newscaster.

9. I asked aloud, Will I miss my dental appointment?

10. We can fight this new fungus successfully, encouraged the biologist. But how? replied the farmers. With basic research and a little luck, she answered.

Copyright © 1983 by Houghton Mifflin Company

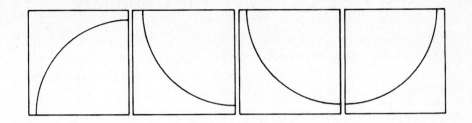

Mechanics

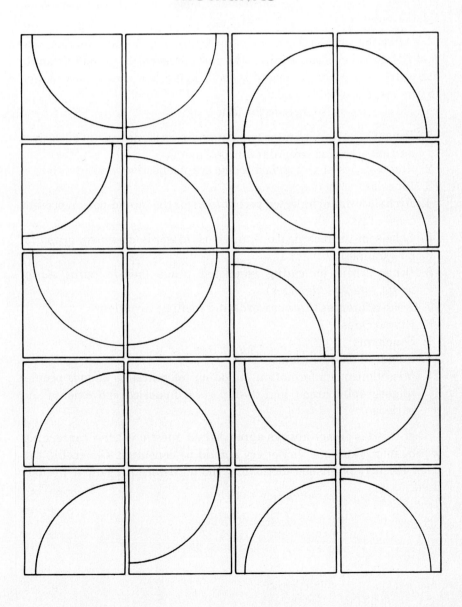

Dictionaries contain information that is necessary for precise writing. The following entry from the *American Heritage Dictionary* for the word *bureaucrat* indicates the kinds of information that are found in an entry. The numbers in brackets have been added.

bureaucrat [1] (byŏŏr′ə-krăt) [2] *n.* [3] 1. An official of a bureaucracy. 2. Any official who insists on rigid adherence to rules, forms and routines. [4]—bureaucratic *adj.* bureaucratically *adv.*

[5] *Usage:* In American usage *bureaucrat* is almost invariably derogatory, unless the context establishes otherwise.

After the word is the following information: (1) the pronunciation and syllabication of the word, (2) the part of speech, (3) the definitions of the word, (4) the ways the word is spelled for other parts of speech, and (5) the way the word is used.

Dictionaries also include the following:

1. Principal parts of regular and irregular verbs, degrees of adjectives and adverbs, and irregular forms of nouns
2. Comparative and superlative degrees of adjectives and adverbs
3. Plurals of nouns
4. Archaic forms of inflected verbs (*doest* for the second-person present tense of *do*)
5. Labels for the technical or limited use of words (*chemistry* or *sports*, for example)
6. Other labels indicating restricted usage (*nonstandard, slang, poetic, foreign languages*)
7. Cross-references to other words and spelling variations
8. Etymologies
9. Synonyms
10. Standard abbreviations
11. Miscellaneous information including references to famous people, to geographic areas, and to important historical movements and periods.

Dictionaries do not always agree. When questions arise concerning words, more than one dictionary should be consulted. Generally, the most recently published dictionary should determine how a word is used.

The Dictionary: Etymologies 13.1

▶ *Using the dictionary find the original meaning of each of the following words.*

EXAMPLE
beret ___*cap, hooded cape*_____

1. oasis _____

2. caddie _____

3. lewd _____

4. noon _____

5. weird _____

6. flaw (defect) _____

7. fang _____

8. glamour _____

9. pupil (student) _____

10. delirium _____

11. trivia _____

12. rival _____

13. travel _____

14. slur _____

15. cabbage _____

16. cabinet _____

17. lady _____

18. buccaneer _____

19. modest _____

20. scuttle _____

The Dictionary: Pronunciation and Parts of Speech   13.2

▶ *Using the dictionary write out the phonetic spelling and list the parts of speech for each of the following words.*

EXAMPLE
brass   *brăs, bräs*   *noun*

	PHONETIC SPELLING	PARTS OF SPEECH
1. scruple	_____	_____
2. jaundiced	_____	_____
3. nerve	_____	_____
4. principle	_____	_____
5. sharp	_____	_____
6. lull	_____	_____
7. spasmodic	_____	_____
8. drudgery	_____	_____
9. harangue	_____	_____
10. curtain	_____	_____
11. aspect	_____	_____
12. August	_____	_____
13. elevation	_____	_____
14. lecture	_____	_____
15. priority	_____	_____
16. success	_____	_____
17. thwart	_____	_____
18. undermine	_____	_____
19. murmur	_____	_____
20. gauche	_____	_____

Italicize (underline) titles of independent publications (books, magazines, newspapers) and, occasionally, words to be emphasized.

Underline titles of books (except the Bible and its divisions), periodicals, newspapers, motion pictures, musical compositions (operas and symphonies, for example), works of art, plays, and other works published separately.

Titles

Books
The World Almanac

Periodicals
Psychology Today

Newspapers
Washington Post or the Washington Post

Motion pictures
Star Wars

Musical compositions, paintings, and sculpture
Handel's Messiah

Rodin's The Thinker

Plays
The Tempest

Names of ships and trains
Underline the names of ships and trains.

the U.S.S. Nimitz

the Zephyr

Foreign words
Underline foreign words used in an English context if they have not become a part of our language. Check the dictionary before underlining foreign words.

The nachalstvo, the privileged class of Russian communist party members, are afforded the same luxuries available to the wealthy in any other country.

Words being named
Underline words, letters, and figures being named.

The word <u>credenza</u>, which now refers to a table, once was associated with poison.

Your <u>m</u>'s look like <u>n</u>'s.

For occasional emphasis
Although underlining for emphasis is permissible on occasion, avoid excessive underlining because it often reveals a writer's weak vocabulary.

NOT

That's not just a big dinner. That's a <u>big</u> dinner.

IMPROVED

That's not just a big dinner. That's a feast.

Italics 14.1

▶ *Underline words that should be italicized in the following sentences.*

EXAMPLE

<u>Sanford</u> <u>and</u> <u>Son</u> continues as a favorite rerun.

1. The U.S.S. Carl Vinson was launched recently at Newport News, Virginia.

2. Newsweek is published weekly.

3. The speech therapist concentrated on difficult consonants like l and s.

4. The word tort was on the latest bar examination.

5. Sixty Minutes is one of the most popular shows on television.

6. Coup de baton is a French expression which means slapstick.

7. Apollo I lifted off and journeyed to the moon.

8. The Today Show has run for over twenty-five years.

9. On Golden Pond won several Oscars.

10. The Wall Street Journal has the highest circulation for a daily newspaper in the United States.

Italics 14.2

▶ *Underline for italics in the following sentences.*

EXAMPLE

Audubon: A Vision is a long poem by Robert Penn Warren.

1. The Southern Crescent, an AMTRAK passenger train, runs from Atlanta, Georgia, to Washington, D.C.

2. A splendid and readable general history of the United States is The Oxford History of the American People.

3. Up from Slavery, by George Washington Carver, is a classic American autobiography.

4. Time had a recent cover story on women's fashions.

5. A Reader's Guide to Periodical Literature is helpful for almost any research project.

6. A favorite science magazine is Scientific American.

7. A spy who infiltrates an organization to induce its members to become involved in criminal acts is called an agent provocateur.

8. The movie Gone with the Wind is based on a novel by Margaret Mitchell.

9. I have trouble with conjunctions like whereas, although, and since.

10. The New York Times Review of Books is an excellent source of book reviews.

Spell correctly. Use the dictionary when you are uncertain of the spelling.

Be particularly careful of words that are not spelled as they sound (*though* and *debt*), words that sound the same (*sew* and *so*), words with the "uh" sound, which gives no clue to their spelling (*terrible* and *persistent*).

Do not misspell words by omitting a syllable that is occasionally not pronounced (*accidently* for *accidentally*), by adding syllables (*mischievious* for *mischievous*), or by changing syllables (*preform* for *perform*).

Guides for spelling

For *ie* and *ei*
Use *i* before *e (believe)* except after *c (receive)* or when these letters are sounded as *a (neighbor)*. There are a few exceptions *(either, neither, leisure, seize, weird, height)*.

Final *e*
Drop the final *e* when adding a **suffix** if the suffix begins with a vowel *(dine* to *dining)*. Keep the *e* if the suffix begins with a consonant (*leave* to *leaving*). There are some exceptions (for example, *notice* becomes *noticeable,* and *awe* becomes *awful.*)

For changing *y* to *i*
Change the *y* to *i* when the *y* is preceded by a consonant, but not when the *y* is preceded by a vowel or when *-ing* is added (*story* become *stories, delay* becomes *delays,* and *fly* becomes *flying*).

Suffixes
If the suffix begins with a consonant, do not double the final consonant of a word (*quick* becomes *quickly*). If the suffix begins with a vowel, double the last consonant of one-syllable words (*bat* becomes *batting*) and of words of more than one syllable if the accent is on the last syllable (*occúr* becomes *occurrence*). Do not double the final consonant if that consonant is preceded by two vowels (*repair* becomes *repairing*), or if the word ends with two or more consonants (*drink* becomes *drinking*), or if the last syllable of the word is not pronounced after the suffix is added (*préfer* becomes *préference*).

Plurals
Add *-s* for plurals of most nouns (*sound* becomes *sounds*) and for nouns ending in *o* when it is preceded by a vowel (*portfolio* becomes *portfolios*). Add *-es* when the plural has another syllable that is pronounced (*speech*

becomes *speeches*) and in most cases when the noun ends in *o* preceded by a consonant (*tomato* becomes *tomatoes*). See a dictionary for the exceptions.

The plurals of proper names are generally formed by adding *-s* or *-es* (*Taylor, Taylors; Jones, Joneses*).

Hyphenation and syllabication

Use a hyphen in certain compound words and in words divided at the end of a line.

It is best to consult a dictionary to determine whether a compound word is hyphenated or is written as one or two words. Hyphenate a compound of two or more words used as a single modifier before a noun.

HYPHEN	NO HYPHEN
He is a *well-known* millionaire.	The millionaire is *well known*.

Hyphenate spelled-out compound numbers from *twenty-one* through *ninety-nine*.

When hyphenating a word at the end of a line, do not divide one-syllable words, do not put a one-letter syllable on a separate line (*a-long,* for example) and avoid carrying over a two-letter suffix to another line (*pock-et*). Divide words according to the syllabication in the dictionary.

Spelling: Suffixes   15.2

▶ *In the blank spaces provided, write the correct spellings of the following words.*

EXAMPLE

stop / ing ___*stopping*___

1. transfer / ing _____

2. cope / ing _____

3. keen / ness _____

4. murder / ous ___*rn*___

5. slave / ish ___*slavish*___

9. wishful / ly ___*wishfully*___

7. transfer / able _____

8. cater / er ___*caterer*___

9. business / like _____

10. solid / ly ___*solidly*___

11. scarce / ity ___*scarcity*___

12. compensate / ion _____

13. sale / able ___*saleable*___

14. sole / ly ___*solely*___

15. treasure / ed ___*treasured*___

16. solid / ify ___*solidify*___

17. tolerate / ion ___*toleration*___

18. blandish / ment ___*blandishment*___

19. traitor / ous ___*traitorous*___

20. season / able ___*seasonable*___

21. alter / able ___*alterable*___

22. resign / ation _____ *resignation* _____

23. foresee / able _____ *foreseeable* _____

24. attribute / ion _____ *attribution* _____

25. create / ion _____ *creation* _____

Spelling: *ie* and *ei*   **15.3**

▶ *Fill in the blanks in the following words with* ie *or* ei.

EXAMPLE
defic _ie_ nt

1. retr _ie_ ve
2. w _ei_ rd
3. conc _ei_ ve
4. al _ie_ n
5. m _ie_ n
6. dec _ei_ ve
7. d _ei_ ve
8. r _ei_ n
9. sp _ie_ l
10. sl _ei_ gh
11. conc _ei_ t
12. Pl _ei_ stocene
13. _Ei_ nst _ei_ n
14. _ei_ ghty
15. _ei_ ffel
16. rec _ei_ ve
17. bel _ie_ ve
18. fr _ie_ nd
19. f _ie_ nd
20. repr _ie_ ve
21. l _ie_ ge
22. br _ie_ f

24. r___ei___gn

25. f_ie_f

Spelling: *ie* and *ei*   **15.4**

▶ *Fill in the blanks in the following words with* ie *or* ei.

EXAMPLE
prem_*ie*_r

1. f_*ie*_ld
2. gr_*ie*_f
3. l_*ei*_sure
4. gr_*ie*_vance
5. v_*ei*_n
6. c_*ei*_ling
7. rel_*ie*_f
8. surf_*ei*_t
9. n_*ie*_ce
10. sh_*ei*_k
11. h_*ei*_ght
12. y_*ie*_ld
13. sh_*ie*_ld
14. v_*ie*_
15. burgom_*ei*_ster
16. st_*ei*_n
17. l_*ie*_n
18. f_*ei*_gn
19. dec_*ei*_t
20. rec_*ei*_pt
21. v_*ei*_l
22. v_*ie*_w
23. w_*ie*_ld

24. l __ di __ s __ r

25. p __ ll __ gr __ ir

Spelling: Plurals 15.5

▶ *Form the plural for each of the following nouns. If there is more than one plural form, give all of them. Consult your dictionary when in doubt.*

EXAMPLE
bush _____*bushes*_____

1. datum _____*data*_____

2. potato *es*_____

3. heiress _____

4. locus _*loci*_____

5. tantrum *s*_____

6. entrance *s*_____

7. redundancy *ies*_____

8. redress *es*_____

9. sky _*skies*_____

10. mesa *s*_____

11. isometric *s*_____

12. rogue *r*_____

13. stigma *s*_____

14. travelogue *s*_____

15. manifesto *s*_____

16. ghetto *c*_____

17. moose _____

18. medium (referring to communication) *s*_____

19. self _*selves*_____

20. tremor *s*_____

21. hippopotamus _____

22. irritant _____

23. fragrance _____

24. scientist _____

25. miscue _____

Hyphenation 15.6

▶ *Write the correct spelling of the following compounds in the blanks at the right. If a spelling is correct, write C in the blank. Consult a recent dictionary.*

EXAMPLE

hat-less *hatless*

reenter *re-enter*

1. self-importance _____

2. bilateral _____

3. re-gain _____

4. mix-up (confusion) _____

5. fast moving auto _____

6. little worn clothes _____

7. day to day activities _____

8. space-age device _____

9. sixty three _____

10. higgledy piggledly _____

11. high water mark _____

12. fore-runner _____

13. left-wing _____

14. long term bond _____

15. public service corporation _____

16. re-new _____

17. semi-annual _____

18. ninety four _____

19. one and one fourth inches _____

20. honey-dew melon _____

21. grassroots _____

22. self defense _____

23. chair woman _____

24. bric a brac _____

25. close out sale _____

Hyphenation and Syllabication   15.7

▶ *Circle errors in hyphenation or syllabication and correct them. Add hyphens where necessary.*

EXAMPLE
Money-market␣accounts are very popular.

1. The date of the revised-memorandum was October 12, 1982.

2. The company secretary put-down the minutes exactly as she heard them.

3. A self critical executive may be a valuable employee.

4. The tender offer was a standoff until last week.

5. For a brief period real-estate-investment-trusts enjoyed great popularity.

6. "Don't shilly shally," Ann said. "Either purchase the option or forget the contract."

7. We visited the Smithsonian-Institution in Washington.

8. Explanation of the new line of soft-ware pre-empted other agenda items for the sales meeting.

9. The police investigated an accident involving a hit-and run driver who had ignored a stop sign.

10. We wanted the disc-jockey to stop talking and play the record.

Apostrophes
Use the apostrophe for the possessive case of many nouns, contractions, omissions, and some plurals.

Use *'s* for the possessive of nouns not ending in *s*.

SINGULAR

child's, worker's

PLURAL

people's, women's

Use *'s* or *'* without the *s* for possessive of singular nouns ending in *s*. Do not add the *s* when a singular noun ending in *s* is followed by a word that begins with *s*.

Dennis's, or Dennis' *but not* Dennis's stories

Use *'* without the *s* to form the possessive of plural nouns ending in *s*.

the Howards' vacation, the actresses' dressing room

Use *'s* to form the possessive of indefinite pronouns.

anyone's, everybody's, neither's

Use *'s* with only the last noun when indicating joint possession in a pair or series.

Elizabeth and Bob's car was new. (They own the car together.)

Elizabeth's and Bob's cars were new. (They each own a car.)

Use *'* to show omissions or to form contractions.

the '80s, won't, it's (it is)

Use *'s* to form the plural of numerals, letters, and words being named.

five *9*'s, three *b*'s

Capital letters
Use a capital letter to begin a sentence and to designate a proper noun.

Capitalize the first word in a sentence, the letter *I*, and the interjection *O*.

What, O what, have I done?

Capitalize the first, last, and important words in titles, including the second part of hyphenated words.

Great Expectations

The Man with the Golden Horn

Slaughterhouse-Five

218

Capitalize first words in quotations and words capitalized by the author.

"We could call this the Age of Indifference," the author wrote.

Capitalize titles preceding names.

Admiral Halsey

Capitalize titles of the leader of a nation even when the name of the person is not given. Capitalize titles that substitute for specific names.

The Prime Minister is in conference.

General Ames has been in Europe. The General has been inspecting NATO units.

A title not followed by a name is usually not capitalized.

The chairman counted the votes.

Titles which are common nouns that name an office are not capitalized.

A private has a hard life.

Capitalize degrees and titles after names.

Alice Trevor, Management Consultant

Denise Lattimore, M.D.

Capitalize words of family relationships used as names when not preceded by a possessive pronoun.

I know Dad will want to see the game.

Capitalize proper nouns and their derivatives.

Paris, Parisian; the Southwest; Democrats, the Democratic Party; the Missouri River; Middle Atlantic States

Capitalize movements, periods, and events in history.

the Victorian Period, the Spanish-American War

Capitalize movements, periods, and events in history.

the Victorian Period, the Spanish-American War

Capitalize words referring to the Deity, to religious denominations, and to religious literature. Pronouns referring to the Deity are usually capitalized.

God, Methodism, the Bible

We know He is our God.

Capitalize the titles of specific courses and the names of languages.

English 101, Mathematics 235

An English course *but not* a Math course (because not specific)

Abbreviations

Avoid most abbreviations in writing. Spell out the names of days, months, units of measurement, and (except in addresses) states and countries.

Monday (*not* Mon.); February (*not* Feb.); ounce (*not* oz.); Fort Worth, Texas (*not* Tex.)

Abbreviations are acceptable before names (Mr., Dr.), after names (Sr., D.D.S.), and with dates and time (B.C., A.D., and A.M., P.M.).

Numbers

Spell out numbers that can be written in one or two words.

forty-five, one hundred

Use figures for other numbers.

12367, $978.34, 3⅓

Never begin sentences with numbers. Rephrase the sentence or spell the numbers out.

NOT
50 men started work.

BUT
Fifty men started work.

OR
There were 50 men who started work.

Use numerals for figures in a series.

We bought 10 pounds of potatoes, 2 quarts of milk, and 2 dozen eggs.

Use figures for dates, street numbers, page references, percentages, and hours of the day used with A.M. or P.M.

USE FIGURES	SPELL OUT
March 7, 1981	the seventh of March
4511 Mary Ellen Avenue	Tenth Street
See page 10.	The book has twenty pages.
He paid 10 percent interest.	
The meeting starts at 10 P.M.	The meeting starts at ten o'clock.

The Apostrophe 16.1

▶ *Give the singular possessive and the plural possessive of the following nouns.*

EXAMPLE
campaign *campaign's* *campaigns'*

	SINGULAR POSSESSIVE	PLURAL POSSESSIVE
1. boss	boss'	bosses'
2. office	office's	offices'
3. agency	agency's	agencies'
4. logo	logo's	logos'
5. employer	employer's	employers'
6. family	family's	families'
7. Smith (last name)	Smith's	Smiths'
8. lady	lady's	ladies'
9. thief	thief's	thieves'
10. Cox (last name)	Cox's	Coxes'
11. Adams (last name)	Adams'	Adamses'
12. minority	minority's	minorities'
13. European	European's	Europeans'
14. employee	employee's	employees'
15. mayor	mayor's	mayors'
16. society	society's	societies'
17. Williams (last name)	Williams'	Williamses'

18. person   _person's_   _persons'_

19. people   _people's_   _peoples'_

20. engineer   _engineer's_   _engineers'_

21. analysis   _Analysis'_   _Analyses'_

22. sister-in-law   _sister-in-law's_   _sisters-in-law's_

23. foe   _foe's_   _foes'_

24. Mendez (last name)   _Mendez's_   _Mendezes'_

25. firm   _firm's_   _firms'_

NAME _____

DATE _____ SCORE _____

The Apostro

▶ *Add apostrophes where necessary and circle incorrect apostrophes.* ⌣
ings where appropriate.

EXAMPLE

Almost everyone's sales increased during the recovery.

1. All the managers attended the seminar.

2. My colleague read our supervisors report.

3. The jobs requirements' included a high school diploma.

4. Womens sportswear is a growing market.

5. The Joneses account is past due.

6. A retailers delight is a long-term fad in clothing.

7. He was trustee of the Perezes estate in '74.

8. My mothers-in-law visit began last week; their's, a week ago.

9. The industrys efforts to change the laws waned.

10. The childrens trust account was managed by a local bank.

223

Capitals   16.3

▶ *Correct the errors in capitalization.*

EXAMPLE
The most populous state is *C*alifornia.

1. The american association of university women holds an annual booksale.

2. My Uncle and Aunt visited last week.

3. My uncle George and aunt Gina plan to retire next year.

4. No longer the tallest building in the Country, the Empire state building remains the most famous.

5. The company's traditional market is in the west and north.

6. Both the south and southeast are called the sunbelt and are considered areas of economic growth.

7. The Steel and the Auto Industries suffer from outdated plants and equipment.

8. The months of Spring in the northern hemisphere are april and may.

9. The Gross National Product is the value of all Goods and Services.

10. A branch manager must follow Company Policy in all phases of the business.

Abbreviations and Numbers   16.4

▶ *Correct unacceptable usage of abbreviations and numbers. Write corrections above the line.*

EXAMPLE   *Twenty-six*
~~26~~ people arrived after 6 P.M., the hotel's deadline for holding reservations.

1. 100's of lawyers are specializing in corporate law.

2. Almost fifty percent of retail sales came in the last quarter of the year.

3. The new management included 2 engineers and three accountants.

4. We invited Sen. Maureen Harris to speak at the conference.

5. At eight in the A.M. the limousine arrives at the corner of 4th St. and 2nd Ave.

6. Over 90% of the sr. class interviewed for employment.

7. T.V. programmers are quite sensitive to public tastes.

8. The van was 200 lbs. overweight and was only eighty-nine % full.

9. The company chose to locate in Tempe, Ariz., and to move the first employees in Mar.

10. Mgt. estimated that the new mall attracted over one million 300 thousand consumers during the 1st qtr.

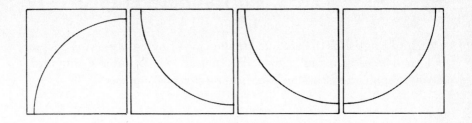

Diction and Style

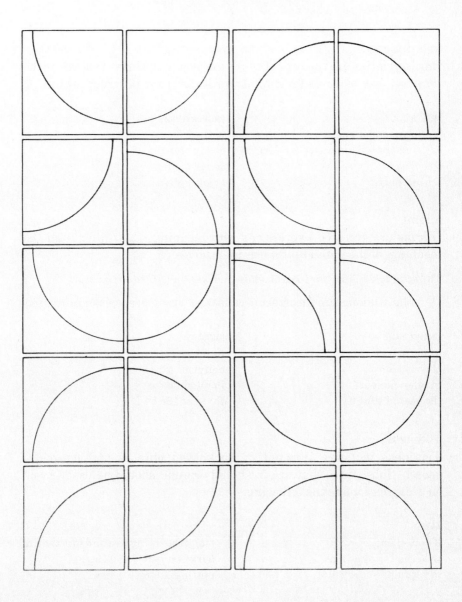

Standard English is the accepted language of English-speaking people. In formal writing, avoid using words that are not considered standard. Always replace nonstandard words in most kinds of prose.

NOT
She was fired up about her new job.

BUT
She was excited about her new job.

Improprieties

Improprieties are the uses of words as the wrong parts of speech or the incorrect uses of words for similar words that have different meanings.

IMPROPRIETY	PROPER FORMS
icc tea (noun for adjective)	iced tea
easy understood (adjective for adverb)	easily understood
except a gift	*accept* a gift
brake a glass	*break* a glass

Idioms

Idioms are accepted expressions with meanings that differ from the meanings of the individual words themselves.

The actor told his co-star to go on stage and *break a leg*. (to do her best)

Many idioms are incorrect because the wrong prepositions are used.

UNIDIOMATIC	IDIOMATIC
conform with	conform to
oblivious of	oblivious to
in reference with	in reference to
the year of 1981	the year 1981

Triteness

Triteness includes worn-out or hackneyed phrases and figures of speech. Substitutes that are fresh and original should be used. Avoid such expressions as the following.

AVOID

if and when	out of the frying pan and into the fire
trials and tribulations	darkness before the dawn
never rains but it pours	putting salt on a wound

Correctness
Correct usage requires a knowledge of idioms, the use of a current dictionary, and wide experience with words. Words must be used precisely; writers must avoid using words that are confusing and vague.

The *astrologer* scientifically studied the moons of Jupiter. (The word should be *astronomer*.)

He was in difficult *straights*. (The word should be *straits*, meaning a difficult situation.)

Wordiness
Wordiness is the use of unnecessary words—words that do not improve the reader's understanding of a sentence. Avoid using many words when one or two will serve.

The envelope containing the electric bill was delivered today. (nine words)

The electric bill came today. (five words)

> Avoid overuse of the passive voice.

The work done by the carpenter was finished. (eight words)

The carpenter finished the work. (five words)

> Revise long sentences to achieve concision.

I wish to say that I have not at this moment fully engaged in this warlike action. (seventeen words)

I have not yet begun to fight. (seven words)

> Avoid dependence on *it is, there is,* and *there are.*

It was John Glenn who first orbited the earth in space.

John Glenn first orbited the earth in space.

There are some medicines that have dangerous side effects.

Some medicines have dangerous side effects.

Repetition
Avoid excessive repetition of words, synonyms, and sounds.

The book on the table is a book about buccaneers in the South Seas.

The book on the table is about buccaneers in the South Seas.

The wind sifted sparks from the sizzling blaze.

The wind blew sparks from the blaze.

Standard English   17.1

▶ *With the aid of a dictionary, label the italicized words (for example,* formal, informal, colloquial, *and so on). Replace substandard expressions with equivalents in standard English.*

EXAMPLE

The businessman *figured* that he could weather the recession by prudent investments.   *informal; concluded*

1. We bought a *poke* of potatoes.   *bag*

2. The personnel director was *mighty* nice to us.   *very*

3. The student thought that studying was a *drag*.   *a nuisance*

4. We thought the plans for the new investment strategy were *crazy*.   *unappropriate*

5. After the movie we jumped in my *crate* and headed for a restaurant.   *car*

6. The unsuccessful salesman was a genuine *doormat,* willing to do anything asked of him.   *easily taken advantage of*

7. My broker had lined up a real string of *goodies,* stocks with great potential.   *investments*

8. We did not know what had happened, but something had gotten his *Irish* up.   *temper*

9. A good tax lawyer should be able to come up with some *nifty* loopholes.   _____

10. Even the corporation president said he got the *heebie-jeebies* when he had to speak to large audiences.   *nervousness*

Standard English   17.2

▶ *For each of the following supply an appropriate expression in standard English.*

EXAMPLE
nuts — *psychotic* _____

1. guy — *man* _____

2. would of — *would have* _____

3. in a bind _____

4. blanked out — *forgot* _____

5. got busted — *got arrested* _____

6. took a dive — *lay down* _____

7. get the dirt on — *uncover the truth* _____

8. dippy _____

9. that's a dilly _____

10. flub — *room* _____

11. He's a simp. _____

12. different than — *different from* _____

13. dope it out _____

14. schlep — *clumsy* _____

15. wonky — *shakey* _____

16. sloppy work — *untidy* _____

17. slap-happy — *silly* _____

18. a criminal's mouthpiece — *criminal's lawyer* __

19. he had cold feet — *he was nervous* _____

20. cool one's heels — *slow down* _____

Improprieties 17.3

▶ *Circle improprieties in the following phrases and correct them in the blanks at the right. If you find none, write C in the blank.*

EXAMPLE

(occupation) hazards *occupational* _____

1. Pulitzer's Prize _____

2. axed the proposal _____

3. a cop-out _____

4. arrested by the fuzz *police* _____

5. a bore speaker *bored* _____

6. a residents requirement _____

7. a lawyer fee *lawyer's* _____

8. a poll vaulter *pole* _____

9. a speak easy *speakeasy* _____

10. a cur coward *despicable* _____

11. an equivocation lie _____

12. He payed the bill. *paid* _____

13. a noisy den *noisey* _____

14. get the goods about _____

15. write correct *correctly* _____

16. to host a friend *host* _____

17. serve ice coffee *iced* _____

18. cruel embroidery _____

19. an inordinate amount _____

20. real easy *really* _____

21. sure tired _____

22. to crimp one's style _____

23. to (altar) one's plans _____*alter*_____
24. to enjoy a feet after the victory __*feat*__
25. The animal is dormer. __*dormant*__

Improprieties   17.4

▶ *Choose the correct word and write it in the blank at the right. Consult a diction-ary if necessary.*

EXAMPLE
Only (two, to, too) species of the cat family are presently facing possible extinction in India—the Asian lion and the Bengal tiger.

two

1. I never use the office (stationary, stationery) for my personal letters.

_____

2. I (paid, payed) my bills on time this month.

_____

3. Without some care, we will probably (lose, loose) this contract.

_____

4. The (principle, principal) of the local school asked our company to make a presentation on ca-reer day.

_____

5. It is important to follow (thru, through) on initial contacts with new customers.

_____

6. We were (quite, quiet) still during the announce-ments.

_____

7. The members of the board will have (there, their) monthly meeting this Thursday.

_____

8. We (past, passed) the crowd that had gathered at the cafeteria.

_____

9. The (moral, morale) of the research team made us certain they would find a solution.

_____

10. The committee was (grateful, greatful) for the support it received.

_____

11. My (conscious, conscience) rarely bothers me when I do something wrong. _____

12. The list of (prescriptions, proscriptions) noting what we could not do was several pages long. _____

13. The (fete, feat) following the national championship victory included a dance and a banquet. _____

14. Monica Astland, the chairperson of the board (proceeded, preceded) the rest of the special guests at the awards dinner. _____

15. The magician was a master (allusionist, illusionist). _____

16. The physicist was noted for his work in (astrology, astronomy) at Mt. Wilson. _____

17. Researchers continue to study ESP, extra (sensory, sensual) perception. _____

18. The (continuous, continual) roar of the huge generators did not disturb the workers. _____

19. The plight of the destitute family (effected, affected) us deeply. _____

20. The new lab technician is thought to be a real (progeny, prodigy). _____

21. From our understanding of the speech, we (implied, inferred) that the speaker disapproved of the new governmental health program. _____

22. Being (an uninterested, a disinterested) party, the lawyer we hired to arbitrate the contract was fair to both of us. _____

23. The state argued (it's, its) case before the appellate court. _____

24. We found (there, their) presentation of the new product extremely dull. _____

25. The author read the (enthused, enthusiastic) re-
    view of his play.   _____

242   Copyright © 1983 by Houghton Mifflin Company

Improprieties 17.5

▶ *Choose the correct word and write it in the blank at the right. Consult a dictionary if necessary.*

EXAMPLE
(There, Their) haste was unnecessary.   *Their*

1. After years of searching, the prospector finally discovered the mother (load, lode).   _____

2. My brother is so (plain, plane) even his wife forgets what he looks like.   _____

3. The bully who lives down the street often (flouts, flaunts) his strength.   _____

4. Discontented employees are encouraged to speak with a (councilor, counselor).   _____

5. At the fair we rode (most, almost) every ride.   _____

6. Donations for the campaign (pored, poured) in.   _____

7. John worked for the Army (Core, Corps) of Engineers.   _____

8. We replaced the window (pain, pane) this morning.   _____

9. The new programmer is quite knowledgeable, but he lacks common (sense, since).   _____

10. We had no (undo, undue) difficulty preparing the materials for the meeting.   _____

11. The river (coursed, coarsed) through the narrow canyon.   _____

12. The police (suspicioned, suspected) the two men they caught a few blocks from the scene of the burglary.   _____

13. We (haled, hailed) a taxi to take us to the airport.   _____

14. The manager had not yet (seen, scene) the monthly sales chart.   _____

15. Jim looked in (vane, vain) for his missing dog.   _____

16. The fire (razed, raised) the old warehouse. _____

17. The salesman looked (pale, pail) when he realized he couldn't deliver the order as promised. _____

18. The accused was read his (rites, rights). _____

19. Uncle Edward always (pealed, peeled) an apple before he ate it. _____

20. Profits (sored, soared) following the improvements made at the plant. _____

21. Finishing the report early was a real (fete, feat). _____

22. My father (reeled, realed) in a large bass. _____

23. When the mechanic was (through, threw) working on the water pump, he closed the hood. _____

24. After the boat sprang a leak, we tried to (bale, bail) it out. _____

25. The (seem, seam) joining the two metal plates was improperly welded. _____

Idioms 17.6

▶ *Circle faulty idioms in the following sentences. Write correct idioms in the blanks at the right. Write C if the idiom is correct.*

EXAMPLE

Presidential and vice-presidential candidates ideally should feel compatible (to) each other.   *with*

1. Tracy accepted the challenge without turning her hair.   _____

2. The hunters froze in their footprints.   _____

3. The two fighters had a real go on each other.   _____

4. He was the maincoil in the efforts to reform the council.   _____

5. The new computer hardware cost our company a precious penny.   _____

6. The new director thought he would never be able to live up with the old director's reputation.   _____

7. Amy decided to divest herself from her stock investments.   _____

8. The stereo I bought is inferior against the one my cousin owns.   _____

9. The surgical team resolved to a course of action.   _____

10. We succeeded on our effort to block the mayor's election.   _____

Idioms 17.7

▶ *Circle faulty idioms in the following sentences. Write correct idioms in the blanks at the right. Write C if the idiom is correct.*

EXAMPLE

This book compares computers (with) the human brain.   *to*

1. Martin was prone of making careless mistakes.   _____

2. Several of my friends tried to dissuade me of making a bad choice.   _____

3. Bill was capable to play any position on the team.   _____

4. We agreed with the plan to eliminate noise in the auditorium.   _____

5. Paying dues promptly is required for all club members.   _____

6. The driver headed down the blocked street oblivious to the warning signs.   _____

7. The burglar was accused with breaking into several homes on our street.   _____

8. Mary is quite partial for cheesecake.   _____

9. The land near my grandfather's house is rich with coal.   _____

10. Our teacher said each student's report had to be done independent from outside help.   _____

Triteness   17.8

▶ *Revise the following sentences to eliminate triteness.*

EXAMPLE
Off the field, the huge defensive end is like a bull in a china shop.

Off the field, the huge defensive end
is awkward and destructive.

1. The advice I received from my accountant came straight from the shoulder because he got down to brass tacks.

   _____

   _____

   _____

   _____

2. About once in a blue moon, I like to put on the old feedbag and live it up at some fancy chili factory.

   _____

   _____

   _____

   _____

3. Whenever Cliff has an ax to grind, he likes to put his cards on the table and strike while the iron is hot.

   _____

   _____

   _____

   _____

   _____

4. I had my report in apple-pie order and planned to turn it in early so that no one could steal my thunder.

_____

_____

_____

_____

5. A person who spends too much time sowing wild oats rarely brings home the bacon or feathers his nest.

_____

_____

_____

_____

6. His crocodile tears did not impress us.

His false sympathy

_____

_____

_____

7. In order to land the new account, I decided to strike while the iron was hot and break the ice.

_____

_____

_____

_____

8. He knew the ropes and was never out on a limb.

_____

_____

_____

_____

9. We took the wind out of the opponent's sails, got their players behind the eight ball, and carried the day.

_____

_____

_____

_____

10. Howard spilled the beans and washed our dirty linen in public.

_____

_____

_____

_____

Triteness 17.9

▶ *Revise the following sentences to eliminate triteness.*

EXAMPLE

Everyone on the team was happy as a lark.

Everyone on the team was pleased with the victory.

1. We told Fred to get off his high horse.

   quit boasting

   _____

2. The manager took the new employee under his wing and left no stone unturned in showing him the ropes.

   under his supervision and showed him

   everything

3. Don't flog a dead horse or split hairs.

   Don't argue about what can't be changed

   _____

4. To save face never wear your heart on your sleeve.

   _____

   _____

5. Howard was on the carpet with his boss because he only gave the account a lick and a promise.

   _____

   _____

6. His stock in trade is taking people down a peg.

   _____

   _____

7. Although the officiating was terrible, the coach decided to clam up about it.

   _____

   _____

8. Agnes was a wet blanket on the picnic because she got cold feet when we wanted to raft down the stream.

   _____

   _____

9. I had to make a decision soon but decided I would sleep on the matter a while longer.

   _____

   _____

10. The sales manager thought she had the jump on the competition, but they were only playing possum.

    _____

    _____

Wordiness 17.10

▶ *Revise the following sentences to make them concise.*

EXAMPLE

~~In her time~~ Marie Curie was one of the most important persons of her age.

1. There are many people who dislike the amount of time the television networks allot to sports.

   _____

   _____

   _____

   _____

2. The music played by the orchestra was enjoyable to us.

   _____

   _____

   _____

3. After looking with great care at the facts, we knew we were prepared to make certain difficult decisions.

   _____

   _____

   _____

   _____

4. After reviewing your application that you completed in our office, we must say that we regret to tell you that you do not qualify for the job.

   _____

   _____

   _____

5. In this age and world in which we live, many people live below the poverty level.

_____

_____

_____

6. Due to the fact that the speaker cannot be present at the designated time, the convocation will be delayed for a brief period of 30 minutes.

_____

_____

_____

7. Another facet of the situation that we must look into is the housing shortage.

_____

_____

_____

8. It is my intention to go to visit the doctor.

_____

_____

_____

9. Under these conditions of unrest and violence, we must institute a curfew.

_____

_____

_____

_____

256

10. There are several workers in our office who are being promoted to higher positions.

Several of our office ~~and~~ workers
are being promoted.

Wordiness 17.11

▶ *Revise the following sentences to make them concise.*

EXAMPLE

I came for the reason that I was hungry.

I came because I was hungry. _____

1. It is unfortunate that ten customers entered the store today, and that was not many.

   _____

   _____

   _____

   _____

2. It is easy to see that this country has witnessed some difficult economic times recently.

   _____

   _____

   _____

   _____

3. It is obvious that my solution to the problem was clearly mistaken.

   _____

   _____

   _____

   _____

4. In the event that a fire breaks out, walk to the exit in closest proximity.

   _____

   _____

   _____

   _____

5. I have never been in agreement with the company's absence policy.

_____

_____

_____

_____

6. In many ways certain cities retained and still do retain a small-town atmosphere in those neighborhoods characterized by unique ethnic charm and lifestyles.

_____

_____

_____

_____

7. He often was accused of indulging in circumlocutions ~~around what he said.~~ (speaking in circles)

_____

_____

_____

_____

8. Throughout ~~the period of~~ his troubles, he was never discouraged.

_____

_____

_____

_____

9. In order to be successful at any job total commitment is required.

_____

_____

_____

_____

10. She is very good at her work, and she is a helpful person.

She is capable and helpful

Wordiness 17.12

▶ *Revise the following sentences to make them concise.*

1. At this point in time, it goes without saying, we are still engaged in finding a solution to the problem.

   _____

   _____

   _____

2. With regard to his health, the doctor considered his patient to be in excellent health.

   _____

   _____

   _____

3. ~~This letter is to inform you that~~ your payment is ~~seriously~~ overdue by thirty-five days.

   _____

   _____

   _____

4. The scientists could only conjecture as to what was the cause of the failure of their experimental work.

   _____

   _____

   _____

5. *Actually*
   ~~As a matter of fact,~~ I left the keys in the ignition while I was shopping.

   _____

   _____

   _____

   _____

6. The plain fact is that I was careless.

   _____ Plainly, I ~~was~~ was careless. _____

   _____

   _____

   _____

7. *At dusk*
   ~~At the end of the day,~~ the farmer stepped down from the tractor and went home.

   _____

   _____

   _____

   _____

8. The wrench on the edge of the workbench would be the right one to use in this situation.

   _____

   _____

   _____

   _____

9. On certain occasions I enjoy lying on the couch and daydreaming.

   _____

   _____

   _____

   _____

10. Late at night I am often desirous of a sandwich.

Late at night I often eat a
sandwich

Repetition   17.13

▶ *Revise the following sentences to eliminate ineffective repetition.*

EXAMPLE

Driving winds *drove* the sailors toward the beach.

High winds drove the sailors toward the beach.

1. The mechanic had three cars in the garage and finished the work on two of the cars.

   _____

   _____

   _____

   _____

2. The lecturer stressed the need to avoid stressful situations.

   _____

   _____

   _____

   _____

3. The infirmary will provide excuses that will readmit students to class.

   _____

   _____

   _____

   _____

4. Floral bouquets for the banquet will be made from flowers in the garden.

_____

_____

_____

_____

5. ~~The art of~~ good conversation begins with ~~the art of~~ listening.

_____

_____

_____

_____

6. Seasonal decorations always brighten the Christmas season.

_____

_____

_____

_____

7. We enjoy working with our financial director because he is the financial director with the most experience.

_____

_____

_____

_____

8. The play was reviewed by a reviewer with little knowledge of theater.

_____

_____

_____

_____

9. We had our roof reroofed by experienced roofers.

_____

_____

_____

_____

10. The electrical system was completely and thoroughly examined.

_____

_____

_____

_____

Repetition 17.14

▶ *Revise the following sentences to eliminate ineffective repetition.*

EXAMPLE

Producers who *produce* useful *products* stay in business.

Manufacturers of useful products stay in business.

1. A total of twelve people came to the party.

   _____

   _____

   _____

   _____

   _____

2. Each and every department head was disappointed with his or her budget for next year.

   All (above "every") ~~his or her~~ *their*

   ~~Each and every~~ department head~~was~~

   _____

   _____

   _____

   _____

3. We put our clothes in the ~~clothes~~ closet when we ~~got to~~ our hotel room.

   reached (above "got to")

   _____

   _____

   _____

   _____

4. The furniture store stocked replicas of many antique pieces of furniture.

_____

_____

_____

_____

5. Dennis suffered through all the trials and tribulations suffered by every new father.

_____

_____

_____

_____

6. Margaret was saddened by the tragic story of the tragic death of a faithful dog.

_____

_____

_____

_____

7. The review ~~of a first novel by~~ a former housekeeper's 1st novel in the latest issue of *Newsweek* was favorable.

_____

_____

_____

_____

8. Marlene endured with patience the aches and pains of her first camping trip.

_____

_____

_____

_____

272

9. The total amount of the cost of their new home was less than they expected.

_____

_____

_____

_____

10. Their inclination to voice their opposition to the proposition on the ballot increased.

_____

_____

_____

_____

Connotation, Figurative Language, and Vocabulary 18

Connotation

Words often have special associations and meanings called **connotations.** In addition, **denotations** of words are their precise meanings. Denotatively, the word *home* simply refers to a dwelling place. Connotatively, the word suggests several emotional reactions relating to family, friends, and special occasions.

Good writers attempt to find words that have the right associations—those that work most effectively.

Fred is a *funny* person. (*funny* is weak because it is too general.)

Fred is *witty*.

Fred is a *practical joker*.

Fred is a *great impersonator*.

Figurative language

Avoid mixed and inappropriate figures of speech. Mixed figures associate things that are not logically related.

He stumbled along like a car in heavy traffic. (Cars cannot *stumble*.)

Use figurative comparisons to create originality.

Language is the cornerstone of civilization. (metaphor)

Opportunity is *like* a good mystery story; you never know what will happen when you turn the page. (simile)

Flowery language

Avoid ornate or pretentious language. Make your sentences clear.

PLAIN LANGUAGE	FLOWERY LANGUAGE
today	in this world in which we live and work
pen	this writing instrument
finally	having reached the termination of this discourse

Connotation   18.1

► *Words which have approximately the same denotation frequently suggest meanings that are different. The combinations that follow bring together words with different connotations. In the spaces at right, rate each word in terms of its favorability of connotation—1 for most favorable, 2 for less favorable, and 3 for least favorable. Be prepared to defend your decisions and to explain the different shades of connotation.*

EXAMPLE

advise _____1_____

tell _____2_____

order _____3_____

1. silly _____   6. wise _____

   preposterous _____   sensible _____

   absurd _____   intellectual _____

2. please _____   7. cherish _____

   delight _____   love _____

   indulge _____   appreciate _____

3. gift _____   8. unpleasant _____

   gratuity _____   terrible _____

   bonus _____   disagreeable _____

4. stare _____   9. sanitary _____

   glare _____   clean _____

   gaze _____   hygienic _____

5. frighten _____   10. cheerful _____

   terrify _____   optimistic _____

   scare _____   sanguine _____

11. reprimand   _____   sale   _____

      rebuke   _____   19. ask   _____

      censure   _____   question   _____

11. mentor   _____   interrogate   _____

      instructor   _____   20. confine   _____

      teacher   _____   restrict   _____

13. cry   _____   limit   _____

      howl   _____   21. evaluate   _____

      wail   _____   judge   _____

14. hubbub   _____   review   _____

      din   _____   22. confuse   _____

      uproar   _____   bewilder   _____

15. late   _____   perplex   _____

      overdue   _____   23. lively   _____

      delinquent   _____   vivacious   _____

16. split   _____   energetic   _____

      divide   _____   24. angry   _____

      tear   _____   furious   _____

17. requisition   _____   irritated   _____

      request   _____   25. large   _____

      demand   _____   enormous   _____

18. transaction   _____   sizeable   _____

      deal   _____

Connotation 18.2

▶ *Words which have approximately the same denotation frequently suggest meanings that are different. The combinations that follow bring together words with different connotations. In the spaces at right, rate each word in terms of its favorability of connotation—1 for most favorable, 2 for less favorable, and 3 for least favorable. Be prepared to defend your decisions and to explain the different shades of connotation.*

1. friend _____

   acquaintance _____

   colleague _____

2. sad _____

   dejected _____

   unhappy _____

3. happy _____

   delighted _____

   satisfied _____

4. festive _____

   joyous _____

   merry _____

5. attractive _____

   charming _____

   captivating _____

6. believe _____

   trust _____

   suppose _____

7. old _____

   ancient _____

   aged _____

8. bellow _____

   shout _____

   thunder _____

9. sympathiz _____

   pity _____

   condole _____

10. comfortable _____

    cozy _____

    plush _____

11. disgrace _____

    disfavor _____

    shame _____

12. crawl _____

    grovel _____

    creep _____

13. scrappy _____

    pugnacious _____

    aggressive _____

14. scrawny   20. male

     lean   mannish

     bony   manly

15. erase   21. impression

     expunge   opinion

     cancel   inclination

16. scheme   22. meticulous

     plan   careful

     arrangement   conscientious

17. face   23. innovate

     confront   change

     defy   renew

18. dispute   24. famous

     disagree   notorious

     debate   well known

19. depreciate   25. scatter

     belittle   disperse

     deplore   separate

Figurative Language   18.3

▶ *Here is a descriptive passage from Charles Dickens's* Bleak House. *Fill in the blanks using the following list of Dickens's figures of speech and images.*

a softer train	peep	pale
rugged	like two beacons	melted
cheerful	glimmered	wandered
		enshrouded

It was interesting when I dressed before daylight, to [1] _____ out of window, where my candles were reflected in the black panes [2] _____, and, finding all beyond still [3] _____ in the indistinctness of last night, to watch how it turned out when the day came on. As the prospect gradually revealed itself, and disclosed the scene over which the wind had [4] _____ in the dark, like my memory over my life, I had a pleasure in discovering the unknown objects that had been around me in my sleep. At first they were faintly discernible in the mist, and above them the later stars still [5] _____. That [6] _____ interval over, the picture began to enlarge and fill up so fast, that, at every new peep, I could have found enough to look at for an hour. Imperceptibly, my candles became the only incongruous part of the morning, the dark places in my room all [7] _____ away, and the day shone bright upon a [8] _____ landscape, prominent in which the old Abbey Church, with its massive tower, threw [9] _____ of shadow on the view than seemed compatible with its [10] _____ character. But so from rough outsides (I hope I have learnt), serene and gentle influences often proceed.

Flowery Language   18.4

▶ *Revise the following sentences to eliminate flowery language.*

EXAMPLE

The inside of a geode glitters with the silvery radiance of sidereal splendor.

The inside of a geode sparkles with crystals.

1. Nocturnal shadows draw near.

   _____

   _____

2. He heaved the bat at the darting projectile.

   _____

   _____

3. The florid barristers displayed forensic aptitude.

   _____

   _____

   _____

4. We observed sparkling astronomical pageantry.

   _____

   _____

5. Two linksters ambulated down the fairway.

   _____

   _____

6. A feline quadruped walked along the street.

   _____

   _____

7. Spring brought arboreal splendor.

   _____

   _____

8. I fondly recall the halcyon days of summer.

   _____

   _____

9. We plunged into the briny deep for our morning exercise.

   _____

   _____

10. The pelting precipitation transformed the pastoral sward into a deep fen.

   _____

   _____

Vocabulary   **18.5**

▶ *In the blank at the right, place the letter of the word or phrase you believe is nearest in meaning to the italicized word.*

EXAMPLE

He has an *annuity:* (a) small summer home, (b) a yearly
payment of income, (c) mutual fund   *b*

1. *amortize* the loan: (a) to write off or liquidate a debt over
   a period of time, (b) to seek friendly relations, (c) to end
   an agreement   _____

2. establish a *trust:* (a) the supporting part of a building, (b)
   management of property or funds by a person or bank for
   the benefit of another, (c) a document describing a forth-
   coming enterprise   _____

3. the firm's *actuary:* (a) existing situation, (b) one who
   computes insurance rates, (c) working capital   _____

4. *debit* the account: (a) to weaken, (b) to charge with a debt,
   (c) declare an account past due   _____

5. *depreciation* of property: (a) a period of decreasing business activity, (b) aging, (c) a decline in value   _____

6. pay the *principal:* (a) amount paid for an insurance policy, (b) head of a corporation, (c) the main body of a financial holding   _____

7. working *capital:* (a) wealth accumulated by a business,
   (b) total value of goods and services, (c) executive committee   _____

8. *commodity* market: (a) an article of commerce, (b) building materials, (c) textiles   _____

9. to *facilitate* matters: (a) to make easy, (b) to make difficult, (c) to mystify   _____

10. list an *asset:* (a) agreement, (b) anything owned that has exchange value, (c) credit given by banks _____

11. court-ordered *liquidation:* (a) termination of a corporate venture, (b) chemical process, (c) converting goods or other assets into cash in order to satisfy claims of creditors _____

12. a *net* value: (a) profit realized after costs deducted, (b) clause that protects lender's interest, (c) fund with widely varied investments _____

13. to *sever* a relationship: (a) cultivate, (b) cut, (c) maintain _____

14. concerned about *obsolescence:* (a) retirement, (b) loss of value of assets due to technological or style changes, (c) increment in value of assets _____

15. to *galvanize* a group: (a) startle into action, (b) divide, (c) characterize _____

16. pay the policy *premium:* (a) expense above planned costs, (b) rise in price levels, (c) amount paid for insurance _____

17. compute the *overhead:* (a) fixed expenses of a business, (b) top management position, (c) detailed appraisal of property _____

18. meet a *quota:* (a) promotional group, (b) a sales goal, (c) candidate for a job in sales _____

19. *reimburse* him for expenses: (a) reprimand, (b) pay back, (c) pay with interest _____

20. receive an *invoice:* (a) close advisor, (b) past-due notice, (c) a list of goods sent _____

Vocabulary 18.6

▶ *In the blank at the right, place the letter of the word or phrase you believe is nearest in meaning to the italicized word.*

EXAMPLE
He gave a *laconic* reply: (a) heated; (b) ill-advised; (c) concise   *c*

1. a *penurious* person: (a) very poor, (b) very wealthy, (c) humorous   _____

2. a short *recession:* (a) temporary decline in economic activity, (b) a recent economic decline, (c) a fraudulent scheme   _____

3. *vie* for recognition: (a) scream loudly, (b) whisper (c) compete   _____

4. a deep *depression:* (a) steep decline of stock prices, (b) collapse of the bond market, (c) long decline of economic activity with extended unemployment   _____

5. a *temperate* personality: (a) moderate and restrained, (b) easily angered, (c) extroverted   _____

6. a *facetious* remark: (a) imagined, (b) intended to be amusing, (c) creative   _____

7. buy wheat *futures:* (a) group of optimistic brokers, (b) economic forecasts, (c) commodities or stocks bought or sold for future delivery   _____

8. sell *securities:* (a) insurance policies, (b) promissory notes, (c) stocks and bonds   _____

9. the voters' *apathy:* (a) enthusiasm, (b) lack of feeling or opinion, (c) courage   _____

10. *vendor* of merchandise: (a) one who sells, (b) stock specialist, (c) traveling auditor   _____

11. an *obdurate* employer: (a) sympathetic, (b) eager to please, (c) stubborn or inflexible _____

12. a cotton *factor:* (a) any privately held bank, (b) person or company that finances loans based on accounts of business, (c) attorney for a business _____

13. a *delectable* salad: (a) fruity, (b) delicious, (c) rancid _____

14. shrewd *entrepreneur:* (a) business consultant, (b) commercial banker, (c) one who starts a new enterprise _____

15. adequate *collateral:* (a) property for security for a loan, (b) jointly held property, (c) property held in trust _____

16. an *appraisal* of real estate: (a) net worth, (b) estimate of value, (c) good profit _____

17. to *malign* a competitor: (a) speak well of, (b) speak badly of, (c) joke about _____

18. a *dilatory* response: (a) slow or delaying, (b) rapid, (c) provoking _____

19. a candidate's *dossier:* (a) set of documents giving information about a person, (c) complete autobiography, (c) holdings of stocks and bonds _____

20. registered *broker:* (a) specialist in business law, (b) official regulator of a market, (c) agent who buys or sells things on behalf of others _____

Paragraph Unity: Topic Sentences 19.1

▶ *Divide the following passage into paragraphs by inserting the sign ¶. The original passage contains three paragraphs. Underline topic sentences, and in the blanks at the end of the passage, write briefly in your own words the controlling idea of the paragraph.*

Probably nothing would be more frustrating to any ambitious individual than to be placed in a particular slot and seemingly forgotten. Most large retailers, after a trainee has been selected for the executive-training program, are continually monitoring that trainee's progress. Performance reviews may be more frequent than for rank-and-file employees. Counseling is usually available. Other perquisites of the trainee are participation in management conferences, recognition by top executives, and the status afforded by being on the executive payroll. Many retailers rotate their trainees rather frequently to expose them to varied assignments, to many aspects of the operation, and to a variety of executives, who inevitably have different strengths and weaknesses, which the trainee can emulate or avoid as he or she develops skills. In addition to providing a better feel for the overall operation, rotation helps ascertain the particular strengths and interests of the candidate. Chains also rotate their executives and trainees, sometimes quite frequently and on short notice. Usually the moves are more frequent in the early years when an employee is preparing for more important positions; later, moves usually accompany significant promotions.

Robert F. Hartley, *Retailing*

CONTROLLING IDEAS

1. _____

_____

2. _____

_____

3. _____

_____

Paragraph Unity: Topic Sentences   19.2

▶ *Divide the following passage into paragraphs by inserting the sign ¶. The original passage contains three paragraphs. Underline topic sentences, and in the blanks at the end of the passage, write briefly in your own words the controlling idea of the paragraph.*

There are several ways of entering most occupations. A pathway to many skilled trades is through apprenticeship programs. Each year some 200,000 are in apprentice programs in this country, and some 40,000 complete the two- to five-year programs. Another way to enter many occupations is to enter trade or technical schools. Many communities have such schools, and they offer both short-term (less than two weeks) and long-term (two years or longer) programs. Another pathway to some occupations is the training provided by industry or government. Some companies select young people for training who they believe will stay with the company for a long time. Automobile companies, airlines, and public utilities, such as gas and electric companies, are examples. In the government programs financed by the Manpower Development Training Act young people can learn skills needed for employment. The military services also provide training opportunities that help some individuals when they come to enter the civilian work force. Another pathway to occupations are the junior or community colleges and four-year colleges and universities. Completion of a college degree and graduate study is the route for entering most professional occupations.

Bruce Shertzer, *Career Planning*

CONTROLLING IDEAS

1. _____

_____

2. _____

_____

3. _____

_____

Paragraph Unity: Digressive Sentences 19.3

▶ *Write unified paragraphs. Be sure that every sentence is related to the topic. In the blanks at the left, write the number of any sentence that is digressive. In any paragraph there may be as many as three such sentences.*

EXAMPLE

(1) To use a library efficiently one must first learn how books are classified in the card catalog. (2) Card catalogs are located usually on a library's main floor—but not always. (3) Books are listed in three ways: by author, by title, and by subject. (4) Thus if one knows a title, but not an author or a subject, one can easily locate a book.

_2_

A. (1) Any group of successful managers will reflect various personality types. (2) Some successful managers are very autocratic, hard-driving leaders. (3) Others are more democratic and relaxed as they strive for a consensus of employees' opinions on goals and policies. (4) Almost all have good vocabularies. (5) Whether autocratic or democratic, the successful manager has respect for his employees and gladly rewards hard work and innovative ideas.

_____

B. (1) Executive credit cards, often called "gold" cards, offer the holder several useful services. (2) The owner of such a card has automatic travel insurance. (3) He or she has an automatic and substantial line of credit. (4) Hotel reservations are guaranteed for the holders of "gold" cards. (5) To qualify for a card, one needs a relatively high income. (6) In the final analysis, however, prestige, not credit, is the main attraction of these cards.

_____

C. (1) American steel companies are becoming more diversified industries. (2) One large steel producer recently bought a major oil company. (3) Another giant steel manufacturer purchased two large savings and loans. (4) While dropping the term *steel* from its name, still another well-known steel company has bought interests in manufacturers of oil field equipment and firms dealing with financial services. (5) American steel's problems are caused partly by lower-priced imports and partly by high labor costs.

_____

D.   (1) The most expensive city for the international business traveler is Lagos, Nigeria. (2) Rome, Rio de Janeiro, and Moscow are much cheaper. (3) One night in a hotel may cost over $150.00. (4) Moreover, the hungry business representative probably will pay over $50.00 for a single meal. (5) If one rents a car for a week's stay, he or she may pay over $600.00. (6) Finally, a typical night on the town in Lagos may cost more than $350.00 for a small group.

_____

E.   (1) Companies with large sales forces may lease cars rather than buy them. (2) The major advantages of leasing them are compelling. (3) First, the company does not make a sizable capital investment. (4) In addition, it does not pay high insurance premiums. (5) However, it also cannot depreciate these cars for tax purposes.

_____

F.   (1) Medical librarians must have a good working knowledge of medical terminology, of library science, and of office management. (2) They also must be good team players. (3) These specialists need a broad medical vocabulary because they must read and understand patient charts. (4) They should be aware also of state-of-the-art technologies which cut the costs and increase the efficiency of all kinds of libraries. (5) Because they probably will supervise the work of several medical transcriptionists, medical librarians must be trained as efficient office managers who can meld the diverse efforts of many into a cohesive unit.

_____

G.   (1) Public administrators must work in several environments. (2) They first labor in a bureaucratic environment of an array of clerks, secretaries, and accountants. (3) They should be aware of historical trends in their particular fields. (4) Also, these administrators must work simultaneously in a political environment and must be able to communicate effectively with legislators, city council members, planning commissions, zoning boards, and county commissioners. (5) Finally, they must deal with other public administrators in what may be called an intergovernmental environment. (6) For few social problems can be fitted neatly into one administrative niche.

_____

H.   (1) A career in retailing involves much analysis of price setting and adjusting. (2) Retailers often use promotional pricing; that is, they cut prices of sale items to allure consumers to other, regularly priced items. (3) Some manufacturers insist that a retailer follow maintained or fair-trade pricing formulas to prevent the image of cut-rate prices and poor quality. (4) So-called fair-trade laws have been repealed in most states. (5) Psychological pricing accounts for such figures as $1.98 rather than $2.00. (6) With this pricing, the retailer hopes a few cents will be perceived as a large savings.

I.   (1) Recent studies reveal that job satisfaction depends generally on good pay, reasonable security, and decent working conditions. (2) Employers who make special efforts to pay their labor force fair wages usually have less labor trouble than those who do not. (3) While good pay is very important to most workers, they also rank job security as quite important. (4) They find great comfort in knowing that their jobs will be available tomorrow. (5) Good working conditions are invariably mentioned by workers as a significant variable. (6) Most desire a clean, neat, safe place to work. (7) Many workers feel that meaningful work is quite important, too.

J.   (1) Several good ways of exploring occupational opportunities include perusing pertinent documents and vocational literature, interviewing others who are already in a particular field of interest, and working part-time in a prospective vocation. (2) Periodicals, brochures, and books on specialized disciplines and professions may give important data on educational and licensing requirements. (3) But talking with those who have on-the-job experience may add practical knowledge that proves to be invaluable. (4) While part-time work in certain fields may not be possible, it is nevertheless an excellent way to gain a realistic perspective. (5) One also may attend a career conference.

Paragraph Unity: Transitions 19.4

▶ *Underline once the main transitional devices (transitional words, repeated words, pronouns, and demonstrative adjectives) that enable the reader to see connections between clauses and sentences. Underline twice those that enable the reader to see the connections between paragraphs.*

A good source of information about the work done in an occupation and what is needed to do it are the people who work in that occupation. In talking to a person who is employed in the occupation, at least three points should be kept in mind.

First, workers may not provide objective answers. Usually the bias is not intentional; it simply happens because they experienced the situation the way they did. Some workers, however, stretch things a little or reveal only part of the truth about how hard they have to work, how they entered the occupation, what they actually do, and the satisfaction they get from being in the occupation.

Second, workers may not be aware of the need for workers in that occupation. They may be able to describe the demand for workers in the local area, but their knowledge of the needs elsewhere and the long-range forecast of employment in the occupation may be limited. Third, not all workers are completely familiar with the facts about their occupations.

Despite these difficulties, talking to workers is often a good source of information. Sometimes it is the only source, for printed information about the occupation may not be available. Employers can also be interviewed, and they will be able to add to what their workers have said about the occupation.

Bruce Shertzer, *Career Planning*

Cross-References to the *Practical English Handbook,* Sixth Edition